Surviving Sexual Abuse

KEVIN BROWN

MONARCH
BOOKS

First published by Monarch Books 1998

ISBN 1 85424 398 5

Editorial Office: Monarch Books,
Broadway House, The Broadway, Crowborough,
East Sussex TN6 1HQ.

British Library Cataloguing Data
A catalogue record for this book is available
from the British Library.

Designed and produced for Angus Hudson Ltd by
Bookprint Creative Services
P.O. Box 827, BN21 3YJ, England
Printed in Great Britain.

CONTENTS

ACKNOWLEDGEMENTS

This book is an acknowledgement of triumph over adversity, of healing over trauma, of love over hate, of faith over despair. It is an acknowledgement of a journey I have made. But I didn't travel alone.

This book is dedicated with love from the depth of my soul to my wife, Joan, whose passion, in all senses of the word, has carried me through the most horrific of experiences. She has also loved and claimed my children as her own, in the most adverse of circumstances. As you read through this book and follow the steps I make, know that at every point Joan was with me. My faith in our enduring love for each other, which has faced and survived unimaginable trials and tribulations, has inspired me and made this journey possible.

I am also grateful to Joan's constructive comments on the text, but her most profound response to the completion of this book, this journey, before she ever read a word of the text, was 'it is the most wonderful book ever, because it has brought my husband back to me'.

I commit this book also to our children:

To E – whose strength and commitment to recover and

5

succeed in so many aspects of her life is a constant source of amazement, delight and pride to me. Her spirit is reflected throughout this book.

To S – whose ability to relate so well to people, and to have the confidence to leave home and be independent, testifies that she has not allowed years of being surrounded by abuse to affect her ability to trust.

To C – whose unwavering belief in the horrors that affected her sister and brother, and her own sacrifice of the relationships she had with their abusers, has contributed greatly to the ability of us all to recover. I marvel at her strength of character, and revel in her successes.

To R – whose childhood has been dominated by the trauma and abuse of his step-sister and step-brother, yet whose steadfast commitment to our family life has remained firm. His ability to cope with and transcend the misery, and find his own way, is wonderful.

To E – whose recovery has been long and arduous, and compounded by so many other difficulties, but who is on the eve of an exciting, albeit frightening, new journey. For long he struggled to see a future, and I was often no support. My journey and his are intertwined. May this book inspire his vision and give him faith.

Finally, I wish also to thank Max and Keith for their care and support, and their helpful advice on the contents and structure of this book.

PREFACE

by the Chief Executive of the NSPCC

The book confronts every parent's worst fear. The fear that his or her child will be badly hurt, perhaps permanently, by the actions of another person.

Kevin Brown describes in depth the dilemma faced by parents when their children have been sexually abused. His personal experience is even more poignant in that, firstly, he was a professional working with sexually abused children and their families and, secondly, the people responsible for the abuse of his children were not strangers but female adults known to and trusted by the children.

The book draws upon current thinking and research and confronts many of the assumptions about child abuse. The author challenges the widely held but mistaken belief that children are most at risk from male strangers. Abuse is much more prevalent within the home, perpetuated by parents and other trusted carers. The author acknowledges that all kinds of people sexually abuse children. He highlights the fact that women abuse children but that their abuse is often not treated sufficiently seriously.

In the book Kevin Brown asks questions about the abuse which badly scarred his children and deeply affected his own Christian beliefs. He examines the inability of the child protection agencies to protect children. He describes children's experience of the criminal justice process which often increases their stress and trauma by in effect perpetuating their abuse.

Surviving Sexual Abuse identifies many of the dilemmas that parents whose children have been abused have to confront. The author talks about his own, and his family's self-loathing and anger yet, at the same time, their need to erase that bitterness and to forgive.

He makes a powerful plea for the creation of a different kind of society and a morality in which child sexual abuse is seen not just as a problem for the authorities but as a problem which is everybody's concern.

This valuable book is a stark reminder of the depressing fact that child sexual abuse leaves a lasting mark upon all those affected by it. But at the same time Kevin Brown provides us with a message of hope. He shows that with love and understanding parents can help their children come to terms with the hurt and despair caused by abuse. Together they can build a brighter future: a future in which abused children can reach their full potential and learn to lead full and fulfilling lives.

Jim Harding,
Director and Chief Executive, NSPCC

FOREWORD

The sexual abuse of children is a hot topic in our society today. I write this introduction in a week when vigilantes have made it impossible to find secure accommodation for a notorious abuser, recently released from prison after serving a prison sentence for manslaughter of a child. The fact of sexual abuse of children is difficult enough to come to terms with in itself, but it is made even worse when the newspapers whip the community into a state that combines panic with vengefulness.

It is into this climate of hatred and ignorance that Kevin Brown's book comes, and it is likely to receive a mixed reception. This is a passionate and controversial book that is bound to upset some readers and provoke disagreement and debate. That is precisely why Kevin Brown has written it. Though it is a book that demonstrates complete familiarity with the literature on the subject, it is not what we would call an objective, academic study. It is written at white heat, because the author's own children have been abused. It bears all the virtues and some of the vices of an act of witness and advocacy. Its anger and pain are compelling, as well as disturbing: its argument is persuasive, as well as offputting.

There are three claims in this book that are likely to generate debate and disagreement. Others, closer to the subject, will offer a more professional estimate of what they find here, but the following three claims made by Kevin Brown disturbed me deeply. First of all, he believes that we see only the tip of the iceberg of sexual abuse. The notorious and professional paedophiles who so outrage public opinion are the tip, the bit we see, the area that is brought to our attention. The real problem, the submerged continent, is the abuse that happens in families. I know that statistically a child is more likely to be abused by a close relative or a friend of the family than by a predatory stranger. In this book it is claimed that abuse of children in the family setting is widespread and, by its nature, almost undetectable.

The second claim that disturbed me is the prevalence of abuse by women. Kevin Brown claims that there is such an ingrained public refusal to accept the possibility of sexual abuse by women, that it is almost impossible for children to be believed when they claim to have been abused by women. He is particularly passionate on this subject, because it was women who abused his own children.

The third and most surprising claim made in this book is that the child protection and criminal justice system does not and never can be an effective way of dealing with the problem. He argues that the present system should be abolished because children and non-abusing parents find it destructive and abusive. He is not exactly clear about what should be put in its place, but the most powerful part of the book is its attack on the very system that is meant to protect children.

This, then, is a book that will provoke debate and disagreement. More importantly, it is a book that challenges us to think again, long and hard, about one of the most intractable of human evils.

Richard Holloway
Primus, Scottish Episcopal Church

INTRODUCTION

CHILD SEXUAL ABUSE AND CHRISTIANITY

Do ye hear the children weeping, O my brothers?[1]

The cries of the children would deafen us if we allowed ourselves to hear them. The silent screams of sexually abused children are all around us. But we don't hear them. Perhaps we can't hear them – perhaps we have become immune to that ultimate treachery. Perhaps we can't believe that in a civilised world such degradation goes on around us, under our noses, in our streets, in our churches, in our schools, but mostly, and most destructively, in our families. Surely it can't be happening?

> But the young, young children, O my brothers,
>   They are weeping bitterly!
> They are weeping in the playtime of the others,
>   In the country of the free.[2]

Child sexual abuse happens. And the fact is that we don't hear the cries of the children. Sometimes we don't even hear the cries of the children closest to us, our own children. How can I say that? Because I know, as the father of three children, that I did not hear their cries, did not understand their fears, did not fully appreciate their sorrows, did not conceive that it was possible that my children too could be forced to endure such treachery, such pain. Two of them later disclosed they endured episodes of violent sexual abuse, inflicted by adults whom they trusted. I was their part-time parent, having separated from their mother, who looked after them half the week. And I did not hear their cries.

I was at the time an experienced social worker who worked closely with teenage children. I considered myself pretty good at child protection work, and at helping troubled and troublesome young adults come to terms with difficult experiences. Few of them ever disclosed to me that they had been sexually abused. But this was in the 1980s, when there was only the beginning of an understanding of the nature and extent of child sexual abuse.

So as a professional, looking back, I know now I got it wrong on very many occasions. I wasn't really open to the possibility that children could be sexually abused. And I was absolutely closed to the concept that my children could be sexually abused by adults who I assumed could be trusted to care for them. I did not hear any of these children weeping. My ears couldn't hear it. My eyes couldn't see it. My soul could not believe it.

Three years after my children disclosed their abuse I spoke to my rector. Why has this happened? Is God using my children to achieve some purpose? Is it meant to be that they must suffer so? And that I must suffer so much also as their father?

The Reverend John Farrant was clear in his reply: 'No God that makes sense to me would ever want children to be sexually abused.' But that left me with a problem of major proportions, and John could help me no more. My children were abused, horrifically, over an extensive period of time by many adults. If no God would want this to happen, then perhaps there is no God. For surely God would have intervened. Secondly, if God exists and he allowed this to happen, even though it was not what he would want to happen, where does that leave me? Am I to blame? What kind of father am I? What am I supposed to do now? And how do I explain all that to my children?

Four more years have passed. I have been searching for answers. To find answers one needs to ask questions. I had big questions and I sought big answers. All my basic assumptions about life, as a parent, as a professional, as a person, had tumbled down, so nothing was to be left unchallenged in my attempt to understand how this could happen to me and my children, and – as I began to realise – to so many other children. I also needed to know if and how we could create a society where child sexual abuse did not need to happen. I needed to know whether there was scope to hope.

I offer this book as an illustration of the journey I have been making, and continue to make. I ask questions of myself as each chapter begins, and I offer some answers, which are both fundamental and controversial. But I never wanted to have cause to write this book. I didn't want the questions, I didn't want to have to find the answers. I feel I have a mission I did not choose but that was thrust upon me in a blunt, brutal way.

I am a different man from the one who did not hear his children weeping. I cannot unknow the horrors of the world, although I still desperately wish I could at times. I can only set about trying to change the way the world is. And, like all changes, they are experienced and undertaken at a personal level. This, then, is in effect the account of my change.

It began by trying to put what I experienced through my children's disclosure of abuse into a context. Why had it happened to them? How many children are abused? Who are all the abusers of children? Why do people abuse children? Why, oh why, could my children not tell me earlier? How could I not realise what was happening? Will they ever recover? How do I help them recover? And where is God when it really hurts, and continues to hurt?

I then was able to reflect on the damage child sexual abuse does to others, not just to children – and in particular to their non-abusing parents and carers. More questions. Will I ever recover from what my children told me? Will I be able to rid myself of my shame and guilt of failing as a father? How do I cope with the abusive experiences I went through during the court case? How do I cope with the abusive experiences my wife and children went through during the court case?

But I also considered what damage is being done to all of us, for in a society based on shared values, with principles of interdependency, the nature and extent of (largely unreported) sexual abuse suggests we carry a collective complicity of enormous proportions. Can our society survive if we expose what is happening to our children? Can we cope with the knowledge that we have created a monstrous way of treating each other? Is such major change, personal and collective, really possible?

Big questions. Sacred cows and established institutions collapsed under my scrutiny, for the complicity is institutionalised, not just personal. I found that the very structures of our society uphold and perpetuate the conditions under which child sexual abuse flourishes. The Christian Church is one of these establishments.

Child sexual abuse is not an issue for a particular profession or agency to resolve for us. It involves all of us, fundamentally. I offer big answers to the big questions. But the solution will depend fundamentally on whether we want to see that there really is a problem. After all, if you've never been arrested by the cries of children, it may be easy to believe there's no weeping to be heard. Or perhaps we assume the children's tears we hear are fleeting and trivial griefs.

I ask the reader to journey with me through this book. I believe it is thoroughly researched, for which I make no apology, even if this makes demands of the reader. Indeed, in no way can this book be deemed light. It deals fundamentally with the darkness within our society and within our humanity.

My initial questions seek answers from the literature of recorded experiences and analyses, written mostly by professionals and academics. I make use of this research to make sense of my own experiences. As will become clear, I find this material not wholly satisfactory in that it provides an understanding of the nature and extent of the problem but does nothing to tackle the cause. I do not bring in questions of God, Christianity and faith explicitly until chapter 7, but when I do it's because I really need to. The answers have not been good enough so far, so I ask more big questions. I find that the Church, in its interpretations of the Gospels, and in its practices, has failed children too.

And it is only when I have examined all these issues that I begin to make proposals for change: in our child care, social norms, legislation, moral codes and Christian understanding.

The outcome of my journey is to invite Christians, who are within or outside the Christian churches, to take a lead. This is not the same as adopting a stance of moral superiority or launching a new inquisition. Indeed, I propose the opposite. I appeal to the basic values and beliefs that we hold dear as Christians, and ask us to examine how we put these into practice in our everyday lives, to support children – all children – in a way that can promote their well-being and reduce the risk of them being abused. For we are all God's children, and no-one possesses us. As God's children we have a duty, and an ability, to love each other.

Christian love is the essence of our being. If we accept we are made in God's image, we can acknowledge our relationship as spiritual siblings – as 'brothers', as Elizabeth Barratt Browning says in her poem. Jesus told the disciples to 'suffer the little children to come unto me', and we too can allow children to reach out to us by making ourselves truly available to them.

We can only begin to make ourselves available if we understand deeply just how much children suffer.

CHAPTER 1

CHILDREN SUFFERING: THE INCIDENCE AND IMPACT OF CHILD SEXUAL ABUSE

My questions

Are my children unique in what they have experienced?
How many other children are sexually abused?
Who are the abusers?
Who is doing anything about it?

The United Nations Convention on the Rights of the Child, the children's charter that has been ratified by most countries, and which has influenced much subsequent legislation internationally – for example, the Children Act in Britain, is failing to change the life experiences of children world-wide. The convention

is being violated, systematically and contemptuously, and no countries violate it more energetically than those who were quickest to sign ... Almost every ill it set out to remedy has grown worse in the years since it was drafted. At the same time, the world has never had more human rights organisations devoted to the interests of children and never have the international agencies proved as concerned for their welfare.[1]

One of these ills, of which there is much media coverage, is child sexual abuse. It has entered the public arena dramatically over the past decade or so, with the names of certain towns or areas now being used to signify controversial cases of multiple sexual abuse. For example, in Britain we have had Cleveland, Ayrshire, Rochdale, Nottingham and Orkney. Fear and hysteria have emanated from the media treatment of many cases, culminating in recent campaigns to remove convicted paedophiles from some communities in Canada, the United States and Britain. In Belgium the investigations continue into paedophile rings which have murdered a number of children. And in England we have been exposed to the lurid tales of children abused and murdered by Rosemary and Fred West, including their own children.

Indeed, the raised awareness of the existence of child sexual abuse, combined with concerns about the possibility of false allegations of physical and sexual abuse of children, has left some adult carers and many professionals – for example, care workers, foster parents and teachers in a state of fear of being around and/or touching children when in direct contact with them in the course of their work. I will address this issue later.

Despite the familiarity of the term child sexual abuse, there is a lack of clarity at times about what exactly it constitutes. An official definition, set out in UK Government circulars, regards it as 'the involvement of dependent, developmentally immature children and adolescents in sexual activities they do not truly comprehend, to which they are unable to give informed consent, or that violate the sexual taboos of family roles.' This definition is open to wide interpretations, and doubtless some people will consider certain activities abusive and others not. Further, certain activities may be considered abusive dependent upon whether they are inflicted by people of particular ages and genders, and degree of closeness with the child or family.

Certain assumptions have grown up alongside the increased awareness of abuse. These assumptions can actually determine what is and isn't abusive, based on the kinds of factors mentioned above. This can then inhibit the disclosure, both at the time of the abuse and retrospectively, of activities that have seriously harmed the psychological development of a child (and subsequently the adulthood of the abused child). Often these assumptions have involved the confusion of love with abuse, and in particular demonstrations of parental love. Fundamentally, these assumptions prevent us from being open to the idea that child sexual abuse may be taking place, and we stop ourselves from seeing and hearing what is really happening.

Beatrix Campbell, in her book on the Cleveland child abuse cases,[2] expresses the enormity and importance of the issues raised when something is done to respond to evidence of child sexual abuse. However, having challenged us to acknowledge the reality of what children experience, interrupt our complacent beliefs, and recognise the politics of sexual crime, she then perpetuates one of the common but (I consider) spurious assumptions of child sexual abuse by persisting with the claim that it is a crime committed almost exclusively by men; and since it is accepted as being a crime that is largely committed within the family, that fundamentally implicates fathers and step-fathers.

Indeed it is correct to claim that child sexual abuse is rarely committed by strangers. Most abuse takes place, regularly and over extensive periods of time, in the child's home. It is perpetrated by those who have the greatest access to children and who are entrusted with the care of these children: parents, other trusted adults and older siblings.

Child sexual abuse is pervasive in our society, as evidenced by retrospective studies of the population (which includes those who now feel able to acknowledge and allow their childhood abuse to be recorded) which suggest that as many as one in four girls under sixteen years and one in eight boys under sixteen years may be the victims of sexual abuse. Abuse continues to prevail after the age of sixteen years: some studies claim that one in three young women have been abused by the time they have reached eighteen years of age. For example, Bass and Davies, who have attracted world-wide acclaim with their book *The Courage to Heal*, state that 'one out of three girls, and one out of seven boys, are sexually abused by the time they reach the age of eighteen'.[3] The Zero Tolerance campaign in Scotland displayed posters in the early 1990s stating that one in two girls will have been sexually abused by the time they are eighteen years of age.

In each study of the incidence of child sexual abuse it is acknowledged that there are reasons to suspect an under-reporting of abuse.

Under the persuasion of such studies we may be more prepared to see the abuse that is continuing to take place. While we are able to come up with statistics indicating the prevalence and incidence of abuse, are we really any more prepared to offer a meaningful response? As Campbell found in her study of the response to the Cleveland cases, the implications of uncovering and responding to the reality of child sexual abuse are vast. The more often child sexual abuse is brought to public attention, the more the outcry against the public authorities for not dealing with it, or not dealing with it properly, or – more usually – for exaggerating the extent to which child sexual abuse actually exists. Alternatively, it may be acknowledged that child sexual abuse may well exist (in the generality), but on this occasion the authorities (generally social workers in social service departments) have acted inappropriately and taken away innocent children from innocent parents.

> It seems that we assign to doctors, the police, and social services a task we can't contemplate taking on ourselves. We demand that they do something. But whatever they do, it seems, causes a crisis. And that is because the sexual abuse of children is a crisis – not out there somewhere but in our midst, in our hearts, in our histories, in our fantasies and our fears.[4]

Abusers are not a relatively small number of unusual, immediately identifiable, perverted adults. They are grandparents, mothers and fathers, uncles and aunts, brothers and sisters. They are readers of this book. They hold all kinds of employment, are members of all kinds of organisations, are from all social classes and races, and they are of wide-ranging ages. They are our fellow citizens. They are among us; indeed, as I will elaborate later, in a sense they are all of us.

Abuse, however widespread, is rarely indiscriminate. Like bullying it is not a random act but part of a power-based social relationship. It is based on a particular kind of relationship, where there is an imbalance of power and where that power is able to be abused. In my work on bullying I have stressed the nature of the relationship issues that create the conditions under which bullying can take place, as well as sustain the roles we all play which exacerbate and perpetuate the bullying cycle.[5]

Child sexual abuse is one form of bullying, and the

relationship issues, both in terms of how child sexual abuse is able to thrive as well as how we set about trying to resolve and reduce its incidence, are therefore equally pertinent. I will introduce the concept of an abusive cycle more fully later, and thereafter identify some of the fundamental factors which I believe are required to underpin strategies for dealing with this form of bullying.

However, how keen are we really to uncover child sexual abuse? For every child who is abused there is an abuser (or more than one abuser). Do we really want to expose these abusers? Do we wish to differentiate between different kinds of abusers?

There is probably just as much physical and sexual abuse as there has ever been. And to a significant extent there has been a major shift in public willingness to be aware of abuse since the 1960s. First, there was the discovery of 'battered wives' as they were termed in Britain, exposed prominently by Erin Pizzey; followed within the next decade by the awareness of 'battered babies' and the physical abuse of young children. Perhaps the turning point in Britain was the case of Maria Colwell who died of her injuries. Suddenly there was public recognition that abuse really did happen in families, and that children suffered. The anger that resulted turned on the statutory agencies, particularly the social work profession, and led to an investment in child protection training for social workers.

In the last decade or so there has been a willingness to acknowledge male-perpetrated sexual abuse of female children, particularly if the perpetrator is a stranger – such as Robert Black who has gained international notoriety for his abductions, sexual abuse and subsequent murder of children within Britain. But this increased awareness tends to be limited to the stereotypes of abuse and the abuser.

In my personal and professional experience I have come across a considerable number of inconsistent practices with regard to alleged abusers. There are many reasons which may explain these inconsistencies, some of which I will address later. However, I consider the greatest and most profound anomalies to lie, first, in the different approach taken in response to allegations of child sexual abuse by women; and secondly, in the response to instances of multiple abuse and multiple abusers.

Child sexual abuse by women

The treatment of allegations of child sexual abuse being perpetrated by women varies from the totally dismissive ('it didn't happen, it never happens') to the minimalisation of it ('it doesn't matter') to the assumption that men must be behind it, forcing the women to commit these acts – the women are victims too. For example, the treatment of Myra Hindley, convicted thirty years ago of child killings in Britain, exemplifies one response to female abusers. She is, on the one hand, seen as an exception, almost a different species, while on the other hand, her culpability may be reduced as she had a male accomplice. The second example is Rosemary West, whose (unsuccessful) defence in court was based on the claim that she was subject to the power and influence of her husband Fred West, who was therefore presumed to be the main if not sole culprit.

Let me further illustrate a range of these approaches to women abusers in actual cases involving statutory and voluntary agencies.

Case 1

A twelve-year-old boy was displaying signs of disturbance at school. His parents had also noticed this, but could not establish why he had become different. Perhaps it was his age? Or change of school? He was eventually referred to the child and family psychiatric service based at the local hospital. This coincided with the school medical service examining him and a set of marks were found on his neck, which were thought to be love-bites. When the hospital-based team questioned him about this, the boy said that he often had such marks. When pressed further he said he thought they happened every time he stayed overnight on his own at his aunt's house.

An inter-agency meeting was called. There was enough evidence and concern that sexual abuse was taking place that a Child Protection investigation was initiated. Therefore the father was interviewed at length about the love-bites, the clear implication being that, since sexual abuse was suspected, he was the most likely perpetrator. He was indignant, and soon all co-operation between the family and the various agencies collapsed. The investigation was inconclusive, although there remained a suspicion of abuse by the father. The boy's behaviour continued to give concern throughout his time at school.

At no time in any of the case records was any further reference made to the allegation that the love-bites occurred when the boy stayed at his aunt's house, or that the abuse might be taking place there, and inflicted by the aunt. This did not feature as part of the investigation. Indeed the case records were quite extensive and showed that there was an immediate leap from suspected sexual abuse (as indicated through the boy's behaviour pattern and the love-bites) to the assumption that the father was the abuser.

Case 2

Enquiries into the conduct of staff in a children's home led to the discovery that a peripatetic male member of staff had interfered sexually with four girls under sixteen years on different occasions over several years. He was charged, prosecuted and – despite the time that had elapsed since the crimes were committed, that he was a 'first offender', and that he was then around sixty years old – he was sentenced to six years imprisonment. At the same time it became known that a female member of staff was regularly having full intercourse with a fifteen-year-old boy in the same unit. She was interviewed by the unit manager, and her subsequent resignation was accepted. The police were not involved.

Case 3

In 1989 a female carer of a fifteen-year-old boy informed her friend that she was having full sexual intercourse with him. This friend was concerned and eventually told the Social Work Department. The carer was interviewed and she acknowledged she had been having a sexual relationship with the boy entrusted to her care. A decision was reached that the boy could no longer reside with these carers. The female carer was very upset about this. She had to explain to her husband why the boy had been removed, and the husband was unwilling to continue in their marriage. There was some sympathy expressed for the female carer: she had lost her husband, and the Social Work Department had dismissed her as a carer. The offence was not deemed to warrant police investigation.

Case 4

In a 1997 British court case a mother who had been having a regular sexual relationship with her neighbour's fourteen-year-old son, and who had stated her intention of continuing in that relationship, was prosecuted, convicted and placed on probation.

The boy's father was indignant. Had it been he who had been having sex with his neighbour's daughter, and who had stated his intention of continuing to have sex with her, he believed he would have been imprisoned for a significant period of time. Part of the reporting of this case suggested that the boy was in some way privileged to be having sex with an older woman: 'every schoolboy's dream'.

A similar case in 1997 was also widely reported in Britain in which a fourteen-year-old boy was abducted by his best friend's mother, Tracey Whalin, and sexually abused by her. They were found in the United States of America, and the woman was charged. However, as the United Kingdom authorities were prepared to deal with the matter, the woman and the boy were flown home. She still faces charges in America, but the reporting of the case in *The Times* (31 July 1997) was typical of the general media viewpoint. Sympathy had been extended to the 'runaway wife', and one report advised that she had a lot of family burdens. Moreover, the boy may well be none the worse for his sexual initiation (although one psychologist was reported as dissenting from this general opinion).

Case 5

At the first British national conference on female sexual abusers (organised by Kidscape, a leading child protection campaigning organisation), Michelle Elliott referred to a child who had come to her organisation alleging sexual abuse by her mother. Three agencies known by Michelle to offer good support to child victims of sexual abuse were then approached. Two of them refused to deal with this child, the first because they denied the child could have been abused by a woman, the second because they had no experience in helping a child deal with abuse by women. Fortunately the third was prepared to offer sensitive support.

Case 6

At the same conference a representative from Childline, the national telephone contact agency that children can call confidentially if they have fears or concerns, acknowledged that they had previously adopted different approaches to children alleging abuse by women to those alleging abuse by men. The speaker then illustrated through a recorded role play how they would *now* approach the child (in this case a teenage boy) who was trying to disclose his sexual abuse by his mother. The tape highlighted the interviewer asking the child what he felt about the sexual activity. The boy was, understandably, confused and anxious. The interviewer gently asked him some questions. Did he like the sexual activity? Did he feel OK about it? What did he want to do about it? The recording indicated throughout that the boy had to work out whether he felt abused or whether he was happy with the sexual activity, and that it was his decision whether he wanted to do anything about it.

Each of these cases illustrates the different perspectives that have been taken on abusive activities dependent on the gender of the abuser. For example, in the last case quoted, is this really the same way that Childline would respond to a teenage girl who was alleging sexual abuse by a man? Or would Childline (and other agencies) adopt a clear moral stand which conveys that the sexual involvement of a female child under sixteen years with a male adult is unacceptable, and is an abuse of adult power? It has been noted that few women suffer serious penalties as a result of their abusive behaviour,[6] although there may be psychological consequences.

Beliefs lie at the basis of the under-recognition of females as perpetrators of abuse. 'Just as we see males as abusers rather than as abused, we see females as victims rather than victimisers. In each case, our beliefs about these gender roles blinds us to disconfirming (and discomfiting) examples.'[7]

Mendel provides a table identifying some of the reasons for the under-recognition of females as perpetrators of abuse, and I pick up some of these points thereafter.

Self-fulfilling assumption that female perpetration is rare or non-existent.

Denial of female sexuality and aggression.

Belief that sexual interaction with older females is benign or positive.

Greater leeway given to females than males in their physical interaction with children.

Greater tendency for female perpetration to be intra-familial.

Greater tendency for female perpetration to be covert and subtle.

Assumption that female perpetrators act under the initiation or coercion of male perpetrators.

'Overextension' of feminist explanations of child sexual abuse as stemming from male violence and power differentials between the sexes.

Politically based avoidance of acknowledgment of female perpetration.[8]

The approach to women in terms of power and sexuality is inherently different from the way men are viewed. Men are sometimes considered *per se* from certain feminist perspectives as potential rapists. No such claim is made about women. So why are women not seen as both sexual beings and potential abusers?

Part of this is due to an analysis which sees social power resting in male control. Men run politics, industry, the legal system, the churches. Male dominance abounds in all the institutions and organisations in society, and in that most intimate organisation, the family. There is much evidence to support this analysis, at least in terms of many of the structures and organisations within society.

But I question just what does happen in families. Who is bringing up the children? Who is left with the child care? When parents separate who usually has the care and control of the children? Even if we accept the analysis which supports the claim that men control their female partners (an analysis recently disputed by surveys of men and women in terms of who actually makes the important decisions within families), to what extent do men actually control what women do with their children?

If it is accepted that men are so dominant in society then we have to question why it is that men have left the control of their children to women. In reality it is the belief system which holds that men are powerful, and sexual, and therefore with the potential to abuse, whereas women are powerless and asexual, and therefore unequipped to abuse, that has created an ideal climate for some women to abuse their children, unsuspected and unchallenged. The hegemony that declares women have innate child-rearing abilities may allow for their abuses to be redesignated as signs of love and affection.

An unfortunate but not untypical reaction when the issue of female sexual abuse is raised is to claim that this distracts from the main culprits and minimises the abuse of children directly perpetrated by men. This is a blatant smoke-screen of the reality of so many children. It perpetuates the lack of credibility in victims of female sexual abuse, and reduces their access to therapeutic or other forms of support. It undermines their potential to become survivors and to recover from their abuse.

I do not wish to underestimate the impact of sexual abuse on children, whoever perpetrates it. I have very real cause not to underestimate it. Therefore I wish to interrupt patterns of thinking and beliefs – in some ways similar to the distorted thoughts and beliefs of abusers, as I will illustrate in chapter 3 – which deny the importance and prevalence of female sexual abusers. My focus is to question the amount of abuse – unrecorded, ignored, denied – that is perpetrated by women.

As far back as 1992, one sexual abuse consultant, Madge Bray, had moved from seeing abuse as being either exclusively perpetrated by males, or perpetrated by females under the influence of men, to reckoning that 'twenty-five to thirty per cent of abusers are women who are directly involved, i.e. women who actively facilitate the abuse of children or who actually themselves commit the abuse.'[9]

Alice Miller also highlights the context for female abuse.

In most societies, little girls suffer additional discrimination because they are little girls. Since women, however, usually have control of newborn infants and toddlers, these former little girls can pass on to their children at the most tender age the disrespect from which they once suffered. When that happens, the grown son will idolise the mother, since every human being needs the feeling (and clings to the illusion) that he was really loved; but he will despise other women, upon whom he can take revenge in place of his mother. And the humiliated grown daughter, if she has no other means of ridding herself of her burden, will revenge herself upon her own children. She can do so secretly and without fear of reprisals, for the children have no way of telling anyone, except perhaps later in the form of obsessions or other symptoms, the language of which is sufficiently veiled that the mother is not betrayed.[10]

I will return later to aspects of Miller's portrayal of both the cycle of abuse and the nature and manifestation of the signs of childhood abuse. Finally, in a powerful attempt to expose the reality of female abusers, Val Young challenges some of our assumptions.

Why is it so hard to believe that some women initiate sexual abuse? As it is still women who have greater care of children, it is they who are the closest and most likely victims of women's sexual aggression. It is true that many such women are out of touch with themselves, possibly addictive, disturbed, perhaps mentally ill, exhausted, depressed, trapped, despairing and frustrated. It is also true that some women who remember later in life that they were abused as children may suddenly recognise that their behaviour to their own children is abusive.

However, it beggars belief to claim that all abusing women are victims of patriarchal oppression and are merely mimicking male behaviour.[11]

Multiple abuse

Moving away from the issue of female abusers, I wish to consider the issue of multiple abuse, which appears to be an equally threatening presence in our society. Some cases of suspected multiple abuse have been well documented in the media, largely because of the inquiries that have resulted from them, and which are now synonymous with the geographical areas where the suspected abuse took place. I refer again to Cleveland, Orkney, Rochdale and Ayrshire, among others, in Britain.

There is a major disparity between the revelation of the statistical evidence (through retrospective studies) of child sexual abuse, including reported abuse by multiple abusers, and the impact when current abuse at a fraction of those statistics is uncovered. In Cleveland only one kind of abuse was being uncovered, that of anal abuse, through the use of the anal dilatation examination (as well as other indicators). The assumption again, of course, was that men (and essentially fathers) were the abusers, through buggering these children, although presumably it would be as possible for women to abuse children by inserting objects anally.

However, the fact that these children (and so many of them) came from respectable homes where the fathers were not in the obvious category of depraved monsters led to a campaign of vilification against some of the medical and social work staff involved in investigation of the suspected abuse. There was overwhelming public disbelief about the allegations. Ten years after these Cleveland abuse allegations, one of the key professionals at the time, Sue Richardson, has had to resign from her current post as she wished to continue to speak out about the issues which arose in the Cleveland cases, and which refuse to go away. It appeared her current employers, National Children's Home Action for Children, who are dependent on the public for their income, feared the possible backlash that might arise from her attempts to remind the public of the reality of Cleveland. It has been confirmed in a confidential Government report that around seventy to seventy-five per cent of the diagnoses of child sexual abuse in Cleveland were accurate, a very high diagnostic figure. This report has not been made publicly available, presumably for fear of the outcry re-erupting.

However, the Cleveland cases did not fall into the usual category of multiple abuse, in that although there were a substantial number of alleged abusers (and victims) the connection between them was not established. That is, there was evidence of a lot of individual instances rather than an organised paedophile ring. In Orkney the situation was different, and a clear link between adults alleged or suspected of abusing children was made. There was also an allegation that abuse involved certain rituals led by a local minister. Suspected abusers in Orkney responded with alacrity. At the outbreak of the allegations of ritual and multiple child sexual abuse by a number of families, which resulted in the removal of these likely child victims into local authority care, an excellently orchestrated media campaign was immediately instituted.

The experience from Cleveland was well learnt, and the opportunity to galvanise public outrage against the Orkney Social Work Department and the Reporter to the Children's Hearing was not missed. As in Cleveland, and as in all cases of multiple child sexual abuse, the public outcry at failure by those agencies charged with child protection to prevent child abuse is only surpassed by the public fury when actions to protect children are implemented. Indeed, in cases where there is a ritual or quasi-satanic element apparent in child sexual abuse allegations, there is an even greater unwillingness to take the revelations seriously. As Ray Wyre, one of the most prominent experts on sex offenders, has stated: 'If you put a goat's head on and abuse a child you'll get away with it, because no one will believe it can go on.'[12]

There is a clear argument to suggest that the incidence of multiple perpetration (and multiple victimisation) is severely *under*estimated, and that the factors inhibiting disclosure are great. Moreover, in all studies of ritual abuse allegations there have been female perpetrators, another factor leading to the dismissal of these allegations as being beyond belief.

Agencies are more than just sensitive to the impact of uncovering multiple abuse. They have an investment in not uncovering it. This appears to me to have been the attitude of a Detective Sergeant and a Detective Constable in one case in which I was involved. They stood in my presence, having heard the most detailed, explicit and traumatic account from two children of violent sexual abuse by multiple adults, including certain ritual elements, and told me they had other priorities over and above those of the protection of other children or the welfare of these abused children. The Detective Sergeant was quite clear he did not want the allegations to proceed. 'We don't want another Cleveland here.'

Such is the very real terror that has entered the world of the child protection agencies. Orkney provided a reminder of why no agency wants to be confronted with evidence of multiple abuse and abusers. The ethos behind the changes in the child protection guidelines following the Lord Clyde report on the Orkney cases has been motivated less by concerns for the welfare of children, and more by the welfare (or even survival) of the agencies charged with responding when allegations are made. Cover your backs, look over your shoulder, keep your head down and your nose clean. And in the case of the Royal Scottish Society for the Prevention of Cruelty to Children, even change your name (to Children First).

This is very understandable. There are numerous professionals so severely condemned by the various inquiries into the handling of abuse allegations that they have gone missing. No Salman Rushdie-type protection, accolades and positive media attention for them. They broke the public silence on abuse. It is they, it seems, and not the abusers, who need to be punished; and, like the example of Sue Richardson, mentioned above, who will continue to be punished if they do not remain silent. As a reaction to this media treatment it has been argued that professionals should be more proactive in speaking out about child sexual abuse, and overcome their fears of litigation, misrepresentation and of breaching client confidentiality. Sarah Nelson, a research fellow at Edinburgh University and a freelance journalist, considers that the professionals' fear of the media has created further damage for abused children. She stated: 'Abusive adults and their supporters use the media as a vital weapon to shape public opinion, and have no qualms about identifying vulnerable children, publishing photographs, libelling professionals and spreading lies and distortion on a wide scale.'[13]

Recently in the United Kingdom there has been the launch of high profile campaigns against child sexual abuse – for example, the CROSS Child Sexual Abuse Awareness month in September 1996, which among other ideas encouraged the widespread wearing of purple ribbons; and the Zero Tolerance campaign against male violence to women and children, which has spread from its origins in Edinburgh to a number of other British cities, and indeed to other countries, with its enormous symbolic 'Z'.

The CROSS campaign has re-emphasised the statistics and emotional damage of child sexual abuse, while the Zero Tolerance campaign has used hard-hitting, uncomfortable images of middle-class violence, albeit perpetuating the denial of the existence and importance of female violence. The overwhelming nature of child sexual abuse being based on an intra-familial relationship is explicitly addressed. However, Mendel considers that 'recognising that sexual abuse is done by those with power, regardless of gender, to those without power, regardless of gender, is, I believe, the next most important step for research into child sexual abuse to take.'[14]

Meanwhile the statutory agencies are being retrained (and sometimes jointly trained, e.g. social workers and police). Changes to the law in Scotland with the introduction of the Children (Scotland) Act 1995, endorsing and reiterating the principles and powers that first appeared in the Children Act 1989 in England and Wales, have emphasised the need to place the child's welfare as paramount. But what will that mean in practice? For at the same time these Acts have re-emphasised the principles that the child should remain in the care of its parents and that no order should be made unless it will lead to a clear improvement in the child's welfare.

We cannot pretend that there has been a significant reduction in child sexual abuse in England and Wales as a consequence of the passing of the Children Act 1989. Nor, as I will argue later, can we hope to achieve any change in the relationships between adults and children, or the conduct of family life, or the care of our children, by pursuing a legalistic approach to child care and child sexual abuse. A much more fundamental approach is required.

I began this chapter by raising questions and quoting from Elizabeth Barratt Browning's poem. Exploring the evidence in order to answer my questions has convinced me that there is real cause for a great many children to weep. These children are in every village and town, in every school, in every street. Ordinary children in ordinary homes. We need to be able and willing to hear them, by tuning our hearts and minds to their reality. We need to believe that they may have been sexually abused.

CHAPTER 2

RECOGNISING THE SIGNS

My questions

How do we know if a child has been sexually abused?
How did I not realise my children were being sexually abused?
Why couldn't I see what was happening to them?
What should I have been looking for?

The usual term for a child who has been sexually abused is 'victim'. So it is a reasonable presumption that if we are concerned that a child has been sexually abused we look for signs of victim-type behaviour; or, as a corollary, if we see victim-type behaviour in children we can presume there may be some abuse.

What do victims look like? Or, to be more precise, what are the indications and evidence of victim-type behaviour? What are the signs?

This is a compilation of signs and indicators that I have gleaned from various sources:

- Abusing drugs
- Bullying
- Constantly blaming self or others
- Eating disorders
- Giving up: 'can't be bothered', 'it doesn't matter'
- Inappropriate sexual awareness
- Isolation
- Obsequiousness

- Preoccupation
- Promiscuity
- Sabotaging friendships
- Seeking attention
- Self-loathing
- Sleep disturbances
- Stealing
- Tiredness/lethargy
- Unwillingness to undress

- Anger
- Confusion
- Depression

- Excessive fear
- Illness

- Insecurity

- Low self-esteem
- Obsessive/neurotic behaviour
- Pregnancy
- Public masturbastion
- Sadness
- Self-harming
- Sexualised behaviour
- Speech disorder
- Telling lies
- Underachievement
- Withdrawal

This is a comprehensive list of behaviour, and it is noted that sexually abused children may only display one or two of these traits. Some of the indicators are more striking than others. Whereas all may suggest some kind of emotional distress or disturbance, some appear to be of an explicitly sexual nature. However, many are not so specific. Indeed, some are rather vague, general, and – let's face it – frequently displayed by most children and most adults.

This catalogue of behaviour is drawn from studies of sexually abused children of all ages, and it is reasonable to examine how helpful it actually is. In particular, the implication that these forms of behaviour are signs of child sexual abuse, that the child is a 'victim', must be placed alongside a general awareness of child development. A toddler who constantly seeks attention may be searching for reassurance or checking out the trustworthiness of the adult caretakers, perhaps as a reaction to the birth of a sibling, a move of house, or a disturbing medical treatment such as a vaccination. Or there may be no obvious connection, the behaviour being an appropriate response to the child's stage of intellectual, emotional and physical growth.

Moreover, there is another problem with accepting this catalogue of signs as indicators of child sexual abuse. Some sexually abused children do not display any of these behavioural indicators – there are no apparent signs of abuse at all. Indeed, there may be a different reaction to the abuse, which leads children to focus and excel in some particular area. For example, some sexually abused children develop a particular zeal for academic study or a hobby, or they commit themselves to perform exceptionally well in sport, music or drama.

Victims of child sexual abuse, therefore, are often extremely hard to distinguish from any other children. Rather than assuming this lack of distinct victim-behaviour to be an indication that sexual abuse has relatively little impact on a child, there is very sound logic for why they should be indistinguishable. The essential human instinct is not to be a victim but to be a survivor. Much has been written about the healing process, whereby victims of child sexual abuse are transformed into survivors. However, I find this terminology somewhat unhelpful, and I will refer to this issue again later. The main problem of this classification in terms of recognising signs of child sexual abuse is that we look for victims rather than survivors. Yet children adopt survival strategies from the moment abuse begins to take place. They have to. Therefore, what we need is an awareness of the survival strategies used by children who have been sexually abused.

There are a number of frequently reported survival strategies, some of which have been eloquently and powerfully illustrated by Mike Lew.[1] These include: forgetting; pretending; denying; distancing; transcending; numbing; rationalising; minimising; justifying; compart-mentalising; striving for perfection; finding faith. I detail these strategies below. The least common survival method is to disclose that abuse has taken place, essentially because to tell may be experienced by the child as life-threatening. I will explore this factor more in the next chapter.

Despite the popular and simplistic view that something as terrifying as sexual abuse could never be forgotten by a child, repressing the memory, storing it in the subcon-scious, is in fact a major survival strategy. The only way to continue to live is by forgetting or, more accurately, repressing the memory of what happened. This has become a contentious area as a strong lobby has arisen around the concept of a 'false memory syndrome' which claims that survivors of child sexual abuse not only could not forget what they later allege they suffered, but also that they may actually invent tales of abuse as part of their history. A further part of the argument put forward by those proponents of the false memory syndrome who have been accused of abusing children is that, had they actually abused children, they too would have remembered it. As this has become a well-publicised 'syndrome', I will explore the evidence for its justification.

In recent years false memory syndrome proponents have organised themselves, for example into the False Memory Syndrome Foundation in the United States of

America in 1992, which was followed in 1993 by the British False Memory Society based in England. These organisations oppose therapists who help their clients find and articulate their repressed memories. It is argued that these memories are false, and that they derive from suggestive therapeutic approaches which encourage patients to redefine their pasts. In the United States of America particularly, but also in Canada, Australia and Britain, there have been legal defences put forward to accusations of abuse based on this 'syndrome'. However, in a study conducted in 1996 of 124 adult survivors, therapy was not a significant part of the reactivation of lost memories of sexual abuse, most survivors having already begun the process of recovering their memories prior to entering therapy. In only one instance was there even the possibility of a 'false memory syndrome' element to the recovered memories, and this was considered by the adult in question not actually to be a factor.[2]

There have been successful defences in court by proponents of false memory syndrome, as, for example, when television programmes have triggered off memories of abuse. It has also attracted some degree of acceptance by a public that is unwilling to believe the nature and extent of child sexual abuse perpetrated within society. Meanwhile scientific research into recovered memory has shown the false memory syndrome to be substantially without foundation, and it is not recognised as a psychiatric condition. Generally it is considered that recovered memories are broadly accurate, albeit with the possibility of some significant errors. However, a working party set up by the Royal College of Psychiatrists in Britain reported its findings on recovered memories in April 1998 in the *British Journal of Psychiatry*. The report, entitled *Recovered Memories of Childhood Sexual Abuse:*

Implications for Clinical Practice, was critical of some psychiatric practices which might induce false memories, and also considered that some aspect of recovered memories may have no basis in reality. Certainly it is clear that memories can be confused – for example, the order in which things occurred, particular facts being forgotten, and significant details overlooked or added – and of course there are individual interpretations of the same event.

However, Alice Miller dismisses the false memory syndrome.

> I have often been confronted by readers and therapists with the problems created for survivors of abuse by proponents of the so-called False Memory Syndrome and by the activities of groups that support 'falsely accused' parents in their attempts to suppress the reports of their adult children. I think these efforts on the part of parents, authorities, and lawyers are motivated not only by the desire to defend their innocence and by financial self-interest but also, and above all, by a much deeper reason: the fear of their own repressed history.[3]

The point Miller is making is that the proponents of false memory syndrome may fear that they too have histories, either of being abused themselves as children or of being abusers, that they have repressed, and that the only way they can continue to live as they did before is to believe that there is no such thing as repressed memory. However, the evidence for repressed memory among survivors is weighty, so much so that Bass and Davies state:

> Children often cope with abuse by forgetting it ever happened. As a result, you may have no conscious memory of being abused. You may have forgotten large chunks of your childhood. Yet there are things you do remember. When you

are touched in a certain way, you feel nauseated. Certain words or facial expressions scare you. You know you never liked your mother to touch you . . . So far, no-one we've talked to thought she might have been abused, and then later discovered she hadn't been. The progression always goes the other way, from suspicion to confirmation.[4]

Bass and Davies, whose writings are the most targeted and opposed by the proponents of false memory syndrome, argue that their experience with survivors has led them to understand that the power to forget is not only one of the most common and effective ways children cope with sexual abuse, but is is also so strong that 'many children are able to forget about the abuse, *even as it is happening to them*'.[5]

Being able to forget the abuse allows a child to survive. If the abuse isn't remembered, it didn't happen, and the child doesn't have to do anything about it. As a longer-term strategy this creates other difficulties, as aspects of recall arise often spontaneously – through smell, touch, association of people and places, within intimacy, and so on. But as a strategy to survive childhood it works.

This strategy is used by adults too. Among adult survivors of the holocaust, and other adult survivors of the most awful atrocities, a significant number block out what happened from their conscious memory. It is undoubtedly a strategy used, too, by abusers. Those accused of torture often cannot associate what is being alleged with their recall of themselves, as fellow human beings of their victims, as the testimonies to the Truth and Justice Commission in South Africa illustrate. A woman who has committed the cruellest of sexual abuse on her children may not associate her actions with her recall of herself as their mother. This is a survival technique that may have been used by Tracie Andrews, who was convicted in England in 1997 of killing her boyfriend, having concocted a story that she had witnessed his killing by some unknown man. Many killers claim that they recall nothing of their actions, and it may be the offence is so horrific that they have repressed it from normal memory recall. It is in effect a state of amnesia.

The best way to cope with the enormity of the abuse inflicted is for the abuser to forget it happened. The claims of false memory syndrome proponents need to be placed alongside the evidence that perpetrators and victims of abuse make use of repressed memory to survive. It has been claimed that while 'there is no good documentation for the consistent presence of false memory on the part of victims, there is a great deal of documentation for the presence of false memory on the part of perpetrators'.[6] That is, people don't invent horrors, they repress them.

Children can fabricate an alternative and idealised picture of their actual experience. For example, the child may conjure up a false belief that the abusive parent is the best mother or father in the world. This denial of reality is often accompanied by the illusion of a perfect childhood. While this can be classed as a false memory, the difference is that it is an idealised belief; it is based on a fantasy available to the child whereas an abusive experience is not part of the knowledge – intellectual, physical or emotional – that can be available to a child unless it is part of an actual reality.

Denial of abuse is a common response in children too. Combined with the awfulness of what has happened, the fear of the consequences of relating the abuse, of telling what has happened, will make denial the obvious survival strategy. Children are sensitive from an early age to what it is safe to tell – and what it is not.

Occasionally it is possible for children to distance themselves physically from their abusers – by running away, or by arranging to stay with another family. These are less viable options generally, and dependent on the age of the child and the risks of challenging the abuser that these actions may infer. More often children distance themselves in another way, psychologically, which can be termed transcending – leaving their body during the abuse. Typically children will later talk about how they remove themselves from their body, rising up and over what is happening, and can recall details of what they effectively observed took place, as if they were watching it from the ceiling. They have detached their mind and their soul from their body.

Children may also numb themselves to the abuse that is inflicted on them. In that way it cannot hurt them; they become immune to pain at both a physical and emotional level. A similar concept is that of 'spacing out', as some survivors have described it, of not being wholly there. Given that the abusers are statistically more likely to be the main caretakers of the child – or if the caretakers are not the abusers, then as caretakers they have still not protected the child from this pain – then the survival mechanism may be to become dead to feelings within the home environment. A dependency on substances and activities that numb feelings can be associated with this survival technique, such as alcohol and drugs, including the total immersion into an interest or hobby, a form of workaholism.

Children also develop the ability to rationalise away the abuse, minimise it and indeed justify it. By so doing children make it easier to accept what is happening, and therefore cope with it. Rationalisation can include excusing the behaviour of the abuser: either 'they know not what they do' or 'they have problems of their own'. Minimising plays down the importance and significance of the abuse: 'it wasn't so bad' or 'it was much the same as any child would get'. Justification can be associated with the type of rationalisation outlined above, but also include a degree of self-blame: 'I deserved it', 'I asked for it', 'I provoked it'.

One of the most effective ways for a child to survive is to compartmentalise the abuse away from other aspects of life. Having separated off the abuse into a discreet, internal emotional and psychological box, the child can then function well in other social settings – at school, with friends, and so on. The child develops separate but coexistent realities, a form of denial and pretence, a disintegration of the whole personality. As a survival technique, it has substantial short-term benefits, but like all these strategies there will be major longer-term legacies of psychological damage.

I noted above that one of the indicators of abuse may not be one of the more obvious signs of distress, but a striving for excellence, in effect for perfection. Sometimes the child may retreat into a fantasy world of the imagination as an escape from the abuse, and as compensation for feelings of worthlessness. Only by being the best will the abused child survive. This too can be associated with another form of survival mentioned above, that of always being busy – the workaholic.

Many adult incest survivors are tremendously talented and accomplished. They have achieved enormously successful careers, amassed sizable fortunes, become well-respected members of their communities, formed deep and long-lasting friendships and relationships, been caring family members, and done great good for humanity. They are, in the eyes of society, successful.[7]

This begins in childhood, through an obsession with achieving success, or the top prize, or perfection in examinations or competitions. However, this is a survival strategy, and still carries the relationship and psychological problems associated with people who strive incessantly for perfection. It may only be in later years that they become aware of the damage this has caused them.

The last survival strategy I will mention is finding faith. When a child's basic belief in their adult caretakers, who appear God-like to the young child, has been violated, it may be important for survival to find another, more powerful entity to place trust in, someone more powerful than the abuser. The child's need for a deity can.be overwhelming. However, this is not always for positive reasons.

Their need for a God can be linked with a child's belief that the abuse was justified, the just deserts for their badness. They must atone for this by becoming more holy in their lives, or work to find forgiveness from God for their part in the abuse. Perhaps they didn't find it wholly unpleasant. Or it may be a yearning for God to magic them better, make them perfect and whole, to provide immediate and complete resurrection. Often it is most important for the child to have a sense of certainty, a simple set of rules, a code of practice, and a creed to follow as the abused child's sense of boundaries may have been completely destroyed. Churches can often provide that structure, that sense of certainty. However, this strategy meets a need for survival, and it must be remembered that some of the critical elements of faith, such as doubt, love and compassion, cannot be encompassed readily within this need.

On reflection I can recall some of the signs that my children were distressed, and some which I missed. There were enough reasons for them to be distressed, such as coping with the far from amicable separation of their parents. It is commonly expected that the break-up of a marriage will lead to significant expressions of distress in the children. What I had no need to conceive was that sexual abuse might be the cause of it for my children. Fundamentally, the signs alone did not provide me with enough evidence and understanding for me to realise what was happening to them. In particular, how could a child who seemed to hold his abuser's hand so willingly, to smile in her company, to express no obvious desire to avoid spending time with her, be the victim of her abuse? How could another child meanwhile be caught up for hours knitting, aspiring to greater competence in her solitary activity? Had I been aware of the survival strategies of sexually abused children, then maybe I would have understood how these were their only ways to survive.

This chapter has sought to provide an understanding of how children cope with abuse, not as victims but as survivors. Whereas all the behavioural indicators associated with victims earlier listed may be classed as clues displayed by children to alert us to their *unhappiness*, all the survival strategies are essentially designed to do the opposite: *to prevent the non-abusing world from hearing the child weep.*

This may give us some indication of the enormous impact child sexual abuse does have on the lives of survivors, and how they may need to perpetuate their survival strategies well into adulthood. Many survivors carry within them traumatic sexualisation, which may be manifested in sexual confusion in terms of identity, norms, and the difference between sex and aggression or affection. Many survivors also feel fundamentally betrayed, particularly if the abuse was perpetrated by trusted adults on whom the child depended, but also if the child disclosed the abuse and was not believed. I will look more closely at the aspect of betrayal when I consider the perception of God as omnipotent parent.

Many survivors, despite their success in surviving, feel a great sense of powerlessness. They have had their wishes, and their bodies, trampled and invaded at another's will. This is a factor that can be compounded by 'personal safety programmes' which are widely operating within schools, and which attempt to empower children, based on assertiveness exercises, to 'say no' to strangers or adults who encroach upon their personal space in uncomfortable ways.

There are fundamental problems in this approach. First, it assumes that an assertive child can significantly redress the power of an abusing adult. And secondly, it takes no account of how the child will recover from having attempted to 'say no' and still ended up being abused. Imagine the impact on a child of such programmes when, faced with their abuser, they assertively state what they want or don't want to happen, and are ignored and ridiculed. The child is not only powerless but will be burdened by a terrible sense of failure, of still being unheard, of not being good enough at asserting wishes, of being unable to work the magic that had been practised in school – compounded by the burden of responsibility that adults have effectively passed from themselves and onto the child for the adults' own protection.

Thirdly, research also indicates that these personal safety programmes are ineffective. When put into a real-life situation, children cannot and do not operate in the way they have been taught, whether the risks involve known and trusted adults or strangers.[8] This could produce another sense of failure for the child – that the lessons learnt were not applied, and that therefore they are responsible for the abuse perpetrated on them.

The fourth kind of major impact experienced by many survivors is stigmatisation. They feel deeply a sense of stigma, of shame and guilt, that they are dirty and bad, and that they are worthless. They can sometimes experience themselves as wearing a badge, announcing to the world that they have been abused. It is as if a bell tolls out as they walk: 'unclean, unclean'.

I have stressed the importance both of the impact on children of sexual abuse, in terms of their identity, the energy they use just to get through each day, and their future functioning, as well as the strategies that they use, successfully, just to survive. This has major implications for how we might create the conditions under which children are able to survive without resorting to any of the strategies outlined, and without being left to dwell in their own world of betrayal, powerlessness, stigmatisation and traumatised sexualisation. While we need to attune ourselves to the possibility of children's distress, we must also enable children to express their distress less silently.

In the next chapter I consider some of the social factors that not only inhibit children's disclosure of sexual abuse, but actually create and perpetuate a cycle of abuse.

CHAPTER 3

THE CYCLE OF SEXUAL ABUSE

My questions

Why do people sexually abuse children?
Do abused children become abusers?
Do we all play a part in allowing child sexual abuse to prevail?
Have I contributed to my children being sexually abused?

This chapter addresses a fundamental question asked by almost everyone who is faced with acknowledging that child sexual abuse exists. It is a fundamental question asked by abused children and non-abusing parents too. It is a dreadful, beseeching question. It wails with the overwhelming sense of pain and injustice. The question, of course, is *why*. The question for victims often comes up as *why me*; and for non-abused siblings it may be *why not me*. My children and I have returned again and again to these questions.

I will begin looking for answers by considering what we know of offender behaviour, based still on very small samples of reported and mostly convicted (and almost

exclusively male) abusers. For example, Williams and Finkelhor, in their study of incestuous fathers,[1] somewhat
tentatively suggest a framework of four factors which, in
combination, may lead to the perpetration of child sexual
abuse. These factors are: 1) an emotional need, which
includes the need to feel power and dominance, perhaps
in a compensatory way for previous victimisation; 2) sexual arousal; 3) a blockage to the meeting of these two
needs in 'normal' ways; 4) a breakdown of inhibitors.

Ray Wyre, Principal Advisor to the Lucy Faithfull
Foundation, has developed a comprehensive framework,
along Finkelhor's lines, in his treatment of sex offenders in
the Gracewell Clinic in Birmingham, England. I have
adapted this framework to see if it can assist our understanding of why (and how) people sexually abuse children.

First, while acknowledging that there is no set pattern
and no typical offender, Wyre has attempted to map out
certain features by analysing offender behaviour into a
cycle. This cycle includes the following elements:

motivation	eg, for power, or to satisfy emotional or sexual needs
sexual fantasy	fantasies can be indiscriminate (male/female, adult/child)
distorted thinking and beliefs	which 'justify' the intended actions
overcoming internal inhibitors	internal controls, self-discipline
targeting	'grooming' a family and a child, making the child feel special
initiating contact	getting time with the child
overcoming external controls	getting legitimate time and space alone with the child

| *overcoming victim's resistance* | by building up secrets which hook the child. |

It can be seen that a family member who is a potential perpetrator, such as a parent or grandparent, will immediately have no problem having legitimate time and space with the child. In that sense the targeting is established, as is the overcoming of external controls. Motivation is a much more significant factor, and has serious implications for how we view children – all children, including those whom we parent. I will consider this issue in more depth in chapter 5, but for the present discussion one point seems obvious. If the parent sees the parental role as being one of legitimate power over the child within the family, and that the child is there to meet the parent's emotional needs, the motivation to abuse is established.

The other factors that remain for the potential perpetrator to work through before fulfilling the abuse can now be considered. These are sexual fantasies, distorted beliefs and thoughts, and internal inhibitors. Wyre presents these factors in three continuums:

If a person has a high level of sexual arousal and desire, and a high level of distorted beliefs and thoughts (which

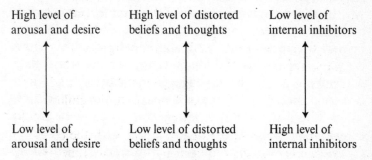

| High level of arousal and desire | High level of distorted beliefs and thoughts | Low level of internal inhibitors |
| Low level of arousal and desire | Low level of distorted beliefs and thoughts | High level of internal inhibitors |

Figure 2

can justify the abusive actions as legitimate), and a low level of inhibitors (internal messages which can induce self-control and self-discipline), then the likelihood that this person will abuse is very high. If one of these factors is at the other end of the continuum – either a low level of arousal and desire, a low level of distorted beliefs and thoughts, and (particularly) a high level of inhibitors – then the likelihood of abusing declines.

Perhaps an illustration of how these continuums may work in practice is helpful here.

If a father – who of course has frequent and legitimate access to his children, which means that one or more of them can easily be targeted, and there are no external controls preventing him having unlimited time and space with them – is unable to get his emotional needs met by 'normal' means, through relationships with adults, and has a need to experience his power over others, he may have the opportunity and motivation to abuse. He may need in particular to have power over his child. If he has little opportunity to express himself sexually with adults, or is unwilling or unable to trust adults sexually (perhaps through being scared of the lack of power he might experience in such relationships), he may have a high level of sexual arousal and desire which he cannot fulfil.

If he then convinces himself, for example, that his children are in effect an extension of his body, in that he helped to create them, and additionally that he has a duty to prepare his children sexually for the world they will enter as adults, he has engaged in distorted beliefs and distorted thoughts.[2] If he has a poor sense of boundaries, which would tie in with his view that his children are an extension of himself, he will have fewer internal inhibitors to abuse. He will give himself permission, supported by distorted beliefs and thoughts, to break the previous self-controls he has exercised. He is in an obvious position to overcome his victim's resistance, and can induce a whole range of emotions in and responses from the child that will ensure compliance and conformity to silence.

I will return to discuss the implications of this approach to understanding offender behaviour later when I make proposals for change. Meanwhile I consider there is another factor which is also relevant if we want to understand why people sexually abuse children. This factor arose out of my work on bullying.

One of the criteria sometimes used to separate aggressive people from bullies is to define bullies as deriving pleasure from causing pain. This demarcation is debatable. While there is evidence that aggression is inter-connected with increased adrenalin, arousal and excitement, there is also evidence that those who consciously and severely damage other people are actually full of self-loathing.[3]

Self-loathing may be more prevalent than generally understood, and may be at the root of many people's involvement in abuse, whether as a perpetrator or as an adult victim (in both cases perhaps after experiences of abuse inflicted on them as a child). Those who loathe themselves, and abuse, may be provoking and inviting punishment. They may want to be caught, to be confronted with the evil they are perpetrating. If their internal inhibitors are so low, they may desperately be wanting external controls imposed: 'stop me', 'help me', 'save me'.

For despite the secrecy involved in sexual abuse, and despite the elaborate grooming process which, as Wyre outlines, offenders sometimes undertake, what we also know is that much sexual crime is perpetrated under our noses, in the light of day, in unlocked rooms, indeed at times and in places where the abuse could easily be discovered. It can of course also be a good camouflage for their actions, a kind of bluff. 'How could I have been abusing a child if someone could have walked in on me at any time? No one would be that daft, therefore the allegation is preposterous.'

However, some abusers are said to experience an extra thrill from the riskiness of their actions. 'Among all the other feelings, the experience is also one of excitement emanating from the surge of adrenalin, which is the physical reaction to fear, a fear rooted in insecurity, despair, disapproval, rejection – in self-loathing'.[4]

The ultimate consequence of insecurity and despair is self-loathing. The ultimate consequence of self-loathing is violence to others or to self in terms of suicide. As a society we need to recognise what this means, as evidenced in terms of the extent of abuse perpetrated. Violence and suicide are the endemic symptoms of a self-loathing society. This has major implications for how we can respond to the issue of child sexual abuse.

A further illustration combines some of the elements of the cycle of offending behaviour with the concept of self-loathing, which in action is the use of a destructive form of power, the expression of emotional despair, which represents the *motivation* within this cycle.

On 13 March 1996, a forty-three-year-old man, Thomas Hamilton, arrived at Dunblane Primary School in Perthshire, Scotland with four hand guns. He entered the school and reached the gymnasium where he deliberately chased and shot dead sixteen Primary 1 children and their teacher. He wounded seven other classmates and two other staff members. He then killed himself.

What could be gathered about the history of Hamilton's life was thereafter widely publicised. He was labelled 'pervert', 'madman' and 'monster' (among other terms). What little we know of him includes the fact that he was brought up by his grandparents where he believed his mother was his sister. His actual father had negligible contact with him as an infant and no contact at all after he was eighteen months old. Thomas Hamilton was a suspected child abuser, although he was never charged with abuse, and may have had just sufficient internal inhibitors to refrain from implementing all of what he may well have been fantasising.

From what we know of his emotionally destructive childhood, we could claim he was an abused child. As an adult he became convinced he was being victimised. There is a suggestion that he had a high level of sexual arousal, and this contributed to his struggle with his internal inhibitors. External controls were mixed – some local authorities refused to allow him use of their premises for his boys' club activities. He had accessibility to boys through his clubs. He did have distorted beliefs and thoughts, expressed through his insistence in a kind of military discipline in his clubs and that the boys should be half naked when engaging in physical activities. His distorted beliefs and thoughts were finally expressed through his devastating actions in Dunblane.

However unique the final actions of Hamilton, he was far from unique in terms of his thought patterns and actions.

There have been claims that abuse becomes cyclical, in that an abused child has a far greater likelihood, bordering on almost inevitability, of becoming an abuser. The case of Thomas Hamilton was a good illustration of how the media sought to explain to the confused, alarmed and outraged public why this man had acted as he had, and they searched for the abuse that was presumed to lie in his own childhood. The claim that there is a cycle of abuse has been based on research of convicted abusers. However, research into the background of abusers is both relatively embryonic and extremely partial. Obviously, unless someone is convicted of sexual abuse, it is virtually impossible to conduct research on abusers. It is unlikely that a random population survey would pick up unknown abusers who were prepared first to acknowledge they sexually abuse children and secondly to elaborate on their own experiences as children.

As we know, a very small and, I would argue, highly unrepresentative group of adults – almost exclusively men who predominantly come from poorer and disadvantaged social groupings – are convicted of child sexual abuse. Most child sexual abuse is not disclosed and most abusers are never charged, let alone prosecuted and convicted, the reasons for which I will address in some detail in the next chapter.

Meanwhile, some studies of convicted abusers suggest a high percentage have experienced physical, emotional or sexual abuse as children (over fifty per cent), while others suggest a much smaller degree of abuse (around thirty per cent) has been experienced by the perpetrators.[5] There is also some debate on whether or not female victims are more likely to turn their abusive experiences inwards onto themselves while male victims turn them outwards onto others – in other words, do women tend to cast themselves, or their children whom they see as an extension of themselves, as victims, whereas men tend to perpetrate abuse on others around them?

Two elements of research are worth noting. Children who kill their parents, who commit parricide, have in the vast majority of cases been subjected to severe abuse by one or both of their parents over a substantial period of time. Most of the children who commit parricide are male, while there is a relatively even distribution of the victims into mothers and fathers. Another factor which may be worth bearing in mind, although it has not been proven to have a causal connection with child sexual abuse, is that suicide is the second highest cause of death of young people next to road traffic accidents. Moreover, recent research in Scotland has shown there is a causal link between self-mutilation and earlier childhood abuse: 'young people who had been victims of earlier childhood abuse were more likely to mutilate themselves and the seriousness of the abuse tended to determine the extremity of the mutilation'.[6]

There is also some limited evidence that there may be a connection between the abuse of animals and child abuse, although not necessarily sexual abuse.

Caution needs to be exercised before drawing conclusions from all these research findings, particularly those based on small samples of abusers. Moreover, the scope and ability for these known abusers to recall and disclose what may have been perpetrated on them as children is a significant factor that would need to be considered. However, research does indicate that where a person has been both a victim and a perpetrator, the victim to perpetrator shift often begins in the pre-adult phase, and there is increasing awareness that adolescents who have experienced abuse are significantly represented in the ranks of abusers. Moreover, becoming a perpetrator of abuse does not mean that the adolescent is not also continuing to experience abuse.

Finally, it does not always follow that, for those who go on to become abusers, the kind of abuse children experience is the kind of abuse perpetrated by them later.

The important factor that arises through this notion of a cycle of abuse is that children who experience abuse of some kind may be significantly more likely to perpetrate abuse as an adolescent and adult. While this has to be a tentative conclusion, it does alert us to the extent to which female abusers may be under-recognised, as the number of female victims exceeds male victims, but the proportions of abusers (reported and recorded) are around ninety per cent male to ten per cent female. The other factor that must be borne in mind is that victims of child sexual abuse may be more prone to being victims again as adults.

It may be well at this point to note these findings and then leave these studies on the shelf, and address the issue of the cycle of abuse from a different perspective.

The impact of abuse on the adult behaviour of the abused child depends on several factors:

- how it has been experienced by the child;
- the extent to which the child has used survival strategies;
- the type of survival strategies used;
- the degree to which both as children and later as adults they find support;
- strategies to help them address and heal their childhood abuse.

It is important, then, to outline the kinds of impact that sexual abuse does have on children in the longer term, as that will give us a reasonable idea of the kind of relationships and parenting that the child will subsequently be likely to engage in. Thereafter I will attempt to formulate a framework which might help us understand the types of roles we play in relationships which make up a cycle of abuse.

I will start this analysis by reproducing a list of patterns, taken from Browne and Herbert,[7] which they have adapted from 'Trauma and victimisation: a model of psychological adaptation' by McCann, Sakheim and Abra-hamson.[8]

Emotional	Behavioural
Fear	Aggressive behaviour
Anxiety	Suicidal behaviour
Intrusion	Substance abuse
Depression	Impaired social functioning
Self-esteem disturbances	Personality disorders
Anger	
Guilt and shame	Interpersonal
	Sexuality problems
Cognitive	Relationship problems
Perceptual disturbances	Re-victimisation
(hallucinations, illusions,	Victim becomes abuser
flashbacks, depersonalisation,	
de-realisation, dissociation)	Biological
	Physiological hyper-arousal
	Somatic disturbances

Figure 3. Psychological response patterns among victims

Apart from emphasising that childhood abuse really does do damage, what this list of dysfunction conveys is that many victims do become involved in some way in abusive experiences in the future, whether self-inflicted, by allowing others to abuse them, allowing others to abuse their family members or children, or by directly abusing others. In other words, the conditions for a cycle of abuse are well grounded.

While there may be a causal connection between being abused as a child and having specific emotional, behavioural, cognitive, biological and interpersonal difficulties as an adult, it is not claimed that this leads automatically and directly to some kind of further abusive behaviours.

Factors that influence the amount of damage experienced and the scope for recovery will be considered in more depth later. It may suffice here to recognise that each victim's experience of the abuse is unique, depending on their personal resources, support systems and survival strategies, as well as being fundamentally determined by the level of betrayal involved. This factor is essentially linked to the relationship between the abuser and the child: the closer the relationship and the more dependent the children are on their abusers, the greater the betrayal and the damage that is experienced.

Childhood sexual abuse is not a random activity. Most abuse takes place within the home, where the child is integrally enmeshed in relationships. Some abusers groom children outside the family, a skilful and laborious process of building up a relationship which is then open to exploitation and abuse. The 'stranger-danger' type of abuse, about which we warn children when we tell them not to speak to strange men, is rare. Children are considerably safer in the street than they are at home in terms of the likelihood of being sexually abused. This factor alone argues that a cycle of familial-related abuse exists, and is more central than an experience of abuse by 'sinister strangers'.

The cycle of abuse is based in relationships and relationship patterns. It is manifested through the roles we play in relation to each other. It involves the use and abuse of power within those relationships. The strength of the attachments to the networks of relationships in which both abusers and victims are located is a vital component of both the scope for abuse and its impact on the victim/survivor.

In my work on bullying I formulated a concept of a cycle of abuse, which I termed the bullying cycle, and which I believe may also be a helpful framework to under-

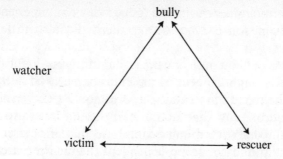

Figure 4. The bullying cycle (simplified)

stand the cycle of sexual abuse.[9] I started with a simple diagram showing the roles that people play in relationship to each other, and compared it to the drama triangle, a tool used in transactional analysis.

In this model there are bullies, victims and rescuers, and watchers who are not *in* the cycle but who are nevertheless an integral part *of* the bullying cycle. Associated with the drama triangle is the concept of the bystander,[10] who literally stands and watches while the drama unfolds. I reproduce below the drama triangle for comparison with this simplified bullying cycle. In each triangle the roles are interchangeable. The fact that it is called a drama under-

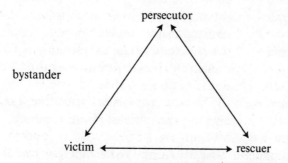

Figure 5. The drama triangle

lines the movement involved – the roles remain constant but each person is able to take them all on at different times.

However, I did not consider that this was a full and accurate enough analysis of the kinds of cycles of bullying and abuse that I have experienced personally and with my own children, and that I have learnt about from my professional work with young people, and that arise from the research and case examples in the literature on child abuse. Therefore I produced the expanded bullying cycle which has the following roles:

- *persecutor*   the person who knows what hurts someone and deliberately does it; who uses the power of force, knowledge, legal position or physical and emotional threats and coercion.
- *victim*   the person on whom the abuse is perpetrated.
- *rescuer*   the person who decides what is best for the victim, just imposes the solution, to 'make them better'; a member of the family or network, or a professional in a statutory child care agency.
- *indifferent*   the person who feels aloof from and uninterested in the persecutor and victim.
- *punisher*   the person who claims a legitimate right to punish the persecutor, to sort the situation out, to impose justice.
- *bystander*   the person who spectates, does nothing, and lets the cycle of abuse continue.

I emphasise that these are roles, not people. People choose to play these roles, but they are not the only ones they can choose. To illustrate how these roles can and do operate in everyday life, I reproduce the diagram which outlines this framework below.

Although there are seven basic triangles within this model, the main point is that all of these roles may be included in the cycle of abuse. The Pu-V-R triangle is a mirror of the Pe-V-R triangle, and deliberately so. The difference between an abuser-type persecutor and a punisher-type persecutor is the moral or societal justification associated with the latter – its righteous basis. In other words the Punisher is the legitimised Persecutor. I will

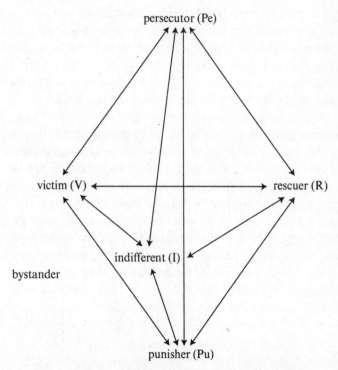

Figure 6. The expanded cycle of abuse in operation

address further issues arising from this legitimation in the next chapter.

Each of the triangles is incomplete. There is a drive to hook in other roles. The Pe-V-R seeks the punisher, who then can seek out the indifferent. The V-I-Pu needs the rescuer, then the persecutor to supplement it further. The R-I-Pu craves the victim and persecutor. The V-I-R will attract the persecutor and then the punisher. *The critical point is that these roles are all unhealthy, all contribute to the cycle of abuse, and are roles with which we may be too familiar.*

And everywhere, everywhere, there is the peripheral bystander – passively waiting and watching and learning, available for any of the other roles requiring to be filled, as well as offering a form of legitimation to the drama that is being enacted. Like the spectators at a football match, the bystanders are as involved in the drama being acted out in front of them as any of the players on the field.

The bystander 'justifications' are extensive. They all explain away the abdication of responsibility. Although the bystander is an unhealthy role, and contributes to the destructive relationships within the cycle of abuse, it can be considered that the bystander role is also a survival strategy. It is adopted by people when it is too painful to take a responsible position. It is a defence against culpability and blame, and it excuses the person adopting this role from intervening proactively and positively. The bystander role is very common, in its various manifestations, and underlines the problem for adults in terms of fear, which I will look at in more depth in chapter 5.

The enormity of the problem to be addressed may now be clearer. As a further indication of the pervasive nature of these dramatic roles, one can listen to the language of popular music and popular fiction. The themes recur. The role of victim – 'I gave you everything and you treated me so badly'; 'how could you do this to me?' And the call by the victim for the rescuer – 'If you don't love me I'll die'. And the rescuer replies – 'I'll love you for ever'; 'I will make you happy'; 'you need me'. Not forgetting the persecutor – 'You will suffer for leaving me'; 'you'll realise what a mistake you've made and then you'll be sorry'; 'you'll be nothing without me'. And the punisher who sneers – 'Who's sorry now?'[11]

This leads me to another one of my questions. How caught up was I in the cycle of abuse without even being aware of it? As parents and partners at home, how do we engage with our family? What messages do we send out? What roles do we play, and want our partners and children to play? What do we watch happening in our neighbourhood, in our neighbours' houses, with the children in our street?

Of course, however much time we spend at home with our families none of us is entirely or exclusively communicating with the other members. We are in transactions with a great many people. In each of these transactions there may be opportunities to be hooked in, or to hook others in, to one of the roles in the cycle of abuse. And we have histories, relationship patterns and experiences that are part of our current make-up, that propel us towards familiar roles.

We are unlikely to be aware of all of this, at least consciously. It may be second nature to us to relate and behave in certain ways in certain situations. For most of us in reality the different roles are virtually omnipresent. And we can and do play several roles at the same time. We can continue to be a victim of abuse as well as a perpetrator (persecutor), as well as a rescuer to another who has been abused, as well as an ardent punisher of someone else who has perpetrated abuse, as well as indifferent (emotionally cold and physically detached) to the abuse that may be being perpetrated under our noses, in our families. And we may adopt the bystander positions: 'washing our hands of the matter', 'not speaking out', 'not getting involved', 'covering our own backs', 'it's none of our business', 'it's their own fault really', and so on.

So what roles did I play? Was I indifferent to my children's suffering? Did I contribute to it by being a victim in an unhappy marriage? I can now look back and see how often I was in a victim role, but at the time I believed my experience of marriage was not atypical. There were times when I played other roles too, particularly that of rescuer (making excuses and apologising for my wife's behaviour), and also her persecutor – ultimately by forming relationships with other women. So in truth I was hooked into the roles, without realising it.

But this may have had an even greater legacy for my children. Not only was I unable to conceive of them as victims of female child sexual abuse, which would contradict my assumptions and my own experiences of parenting, but also I was unable to see what was really happening to my children perhaps because I did not recognise the extent to which they were caught up in the roles of victims, rescuers and persecutors themselves. Now, of course, it is much clearer to me. Of course, I could not have known the nature and enormity of the abuse that took place, but the fact that I did not suspect it has made me question myself deeply.

I can now recall many instances when my elder daughter was showing signs that she was a victim, however well she adopted a stoic strategy to survive. I was aware that my younger daughter was a rescuer of her mother, always concerned for her welfare and happiness, with a script to make her happy – even though I was critical of this rather than supportive of her to escape from that pressure. My son was both a persecutor of my daughters, pinching and biting them, and getting them into trouble, as well as a victim of multiple abusers. It is likely his ability to survive was often in the balance. However, his smile and his public face – a strategy which Sinason has referred to as the handicapped smile, an adaptive response to severe trauma – fooled me into believing that things could not be that bad. Moreover, at a significant point in his childhood his face was painted as a clown, and a photograph taken. It was this photograph that he took and gave to a therapist, soon before first beginning to disclose abuse. Unfortunately, the significance of this photograph was lost on the therapist as it was on me.

> The Joker in *Batman* laughs and smiles all the time. This is not through good humour, it is through appalling circumstances. Thrown by Batman, he lands in a tub of acid and his face is deformed into a permanent smile. He accentuates this with his clown-like make-up. His smile is not one of joy or happiness. It is a manic response to terrible injury. The clown imagery is potent, for the circus clown often relies on pathos, on mimicking the awfulness of stupidity. The clown is often represented with a grotesque smile and a tear at the same time.[12]

My own absorption into these various roles within the cycle of abuse may have blinded me further to their existence when displayed by my children. If being a victim had become for me a normal experience, how could I see it as being abnormal when my daughter experienced it, especially when she had to find a strategy to survive which as far as possible repressed the experience? If my son smiled, how was I to see beyond his public face to see the victim struggling to survive?

So I was a victim, a rescuer and a persecutor within my marital relationship. Was I just a bystander in it all as well at times? The answer is, of course, yes. Yes to all these roles at different times. Some more than others. I was hooked into these roles without realising it. It was extremely hard to become unhooked.

> The cycle of abuse is very powerful, pulling people into it and holding them there. It can be addictive as much as ensnaring. Abusive behaviour is indeed addictive, as the limited research on paedophiles has indicated. Some paedophiles have groomed hundreds of children, and it has become a constant drive for them. It is hard to break this addiction, and there is some evidence that addictive patterns once established over many years, whether substance abuse or person abuse, may never be truly broken. Likewise being a victim can be addictive.[13]

My understanding of survivors of child sexual abuse has deepened, but it has left me with other questions too. The assumption is that those on whom the sexual abuse was perpetrated were the only ones affected. This, in effect, is the notion of victim. But I know it is more complex than this. I recall vividly from my work with young people on bullying how they were traumatised by their experiences of *knowing* that bullying was happening, not even having seen it, and not being the target of it. They were on the periphery of the bullying cycle as bystanders. But just because they were not victims does not mean that they were not affected. Some were deeply traumatised.

I was not sexually abused as a child. However, the experience of my children disclosing their abuse to me, as well as the experience of being cross-examined in court, left me traumatised, and I experienced traumatic sexualisation, betrayal, powerlessness and stigmatisation in the same way as those on whom the abuse was perpetrated. I will return later to consider the impact of child sexual abuse on non-abusing parents, but at this point I emphasise that the feelings and beliefs associated with the roles – all the roles – within the cycle of abuse are negative and destructive. Everyone in the cycle of abuse suffers, including the perpetrator.

There is enormous investment in the criminal justice and child protection systems, in terms of financial resources and personnel, and it might be presumed that this investment is tackling the cycle of abuse. My next port of call on my quest to understand why child sexual abuse is still so prevalent is to examine why the increased knowledge and major commitment through the statutory agencies to protecting children from abuse, as well as undertaking therapeutic work with families, and even specialist work with known offenders, does not seem to be solving the problem.

Are these agencies not open to the distress of children? Or are they immune to it? Are they impotent to respond? Or are they approaching the issue from a fundamentally flawed perspective?

CHAPTER 4

THE PROBLEM OF JUSTICE

My questions

Why don't children tell?
Why does abuse still go unreported, unrecorded,
unprosecuted?
Can the criminal justice system deal effectively with child
sexual abuse?
Can the statutory child protection agencies prevent child
sexual abuse?
Can the criminal justice system break the cycle of abuse?
Is there any justice?

As I stated earlier, there is no suggestion that the level of child sexual abuse being perpetrated is significantly diminishing or that the investigation, prosecution and conviction of abusers is increasing accordingly. The current Zero Tolerance campaign is set to target the criminal justice system in an attempt to seek justice. But how realistic is it to assume that justice could ever be gained through the legal system?

If we accept the retrospective studies of child sexual

abuse as reflecting relatively accurately the current level of abuse, and somehow all the current victims were enabled to report their abuse, there would be an immediate requirement to investigate and prosecute around a million new cases in Britain.[1] This figure does not include incidents of abuse perpetrated in the past, which would further increase the figure substantially.

We know that child sexual abuse happens on a large scale, but within the criminal justice process it is rarely reported, or reported but never fully investigated, or investigated but not prosecuted, or prosecuted but does not result in a conviction. In Scotland the *Daily Record* (9 October 1997) launched a campaign 'in a bid to nail more perverts. Research shows just ONE PER CENT of Scots abuse cases end in convictions'. A two-year study in Hertfordshire, England, produced

> irrefutable evidence that children making allegations of sexual abuse were being systematically let down . . . charges were brought in only 10 per cent of cases, even though professionals believed sexual abuse had occurred in 82 per cent of 148 child protection enquiries. The conviction rate was less than 1 per cent.[2]

The disparity between the numbers who experience abuse and those experiencing the execution of justice could not be greater.

Moreover, despite figures suggesting that an incidence of as many as one in four girls and one in eight boys under sixteen years are the victims of sexual abuse, as stated earlier, or indeed as many as one in two young women under eighteen years, the Child Protection registers held by local authorities in Britain record an average of less than four in a thousand children who are at risk of *any* kind of abuse, including physical and emotional – not just sexual abuse. Some authorities, such as Strathclyde Regional Council which in 1994 covered an area which contained about half the child population in Scotland, had figures of 1.5 children (under eighteen) per 1000 on their Child Protection register. The child protection agencies just do not seem able or willing to recognise the cycles of abuse which lead to such dramatic statistics of child sexual abuse.

If it is a serious proposal that the criminal justice system could and should be able to respond more effectively in dealing with child sexual abuse, even if it is manifestly not doing it, perhaps it is relevant to look at the reasons for the failure of the criminal justice process. I will take each factor in turn. Under each factor I use the term adults to represent abusers, although I am aware as I mentioned in the last chapter that some of the abusers will also be other children or adolescents.

1. Reporting child sexual abuse

First, I will consider the reporting of child sexual abuse. Why is abuse not reported? There seems to be a number of significant reasons, some of which we considered briefly in an earlier chapter.

a) Who does the reporting?

Are we suggesting that, in line with much current (and spurious) thinking on bullying, all that is needed is for a child to tell?

There are many issues at play for a child. For example, how do they know that what is happening is wrong, and how do they know that what is happening to them is not what also happens to all children?

Perhaps they have adopted survival strategies, detailed in Chapter 2, such as repressing the memory of what is happening; or minimising what is happening.

Perhaps they enjoy some of the abuse, or have come to accept it as part of normal life. Perhaps they are told this is a special game just for them. Perhaps they are told it is a secret and it would be wrong to tell. Perhaps they are threatened that if they tell they will be hurt, or more powerfully that if they tell, the adults will harm themselves or be taken away and punished.

Perhaps they are encouraged to feel at fault, to blame in some way for what is happening; it happens because they have been bad, because they have displeased the adults in some way. Perhaps they are terrified to tell.

Even if the abuse has been perpetrated by a 'stranger' rather than a family member or known adult, there is evidence to suggest that a child may find it too hard to tell.[3] Most significantly, they may trust, love and care for the adults. How could they betray them?

b) How can they tell?

How can they tell that they have experienced abuse of a sexual kind? The words and concepts may be strange and uncomfortable. Talking about sex and sexuality is not generally encouraged, even among adults. How can children speak of these unspeakable things?

Their play, their drawings, their behaviour towards other children, adults or towards themselves may indicate distress, sadness or anger. But in a legal system requiring concrete evidence in a logical, coherent, intelligible and essentially verbal framework, what value is put on the way children might try and relate their inner feelings?

c) And whom do they tell?

The people most able to listen to a child are their adult caretakers, primarily their immediate family, and therefore most frequently their abusers. Likewise the child is more familiar with and perhaps more able to talk to the adult abuser. If the trust breaks down, if they can no longer trust the love of these adults, who to a young child will be experienced as God-like beings, in whom can they place their trust?

So to whom else can children turn? Whom could they tell? Who would listen? What would these other adults say, and do if they did listen? What would these adults think about the child who told them about these unspeakable things, who told against the abusing adults?

La Fontaine has summarised the situation:

> Only a fraction of the sexual abuse of children that happens is ever reported. The difficulties of discovering the dimensions of this social problem come largely from the fact that the victims are silent. Or rather they are silenced. For a variety of reasons the victims of sexual abuse as children either do not tell anyone or, if they tell, the information goes no further.[4]

The other factor that must be borne in mind is that children sometimes do tell, particularly about extra-familial sexual abuse, and are not believed. Miles records how one male perpetrator had tried to abduct young girls on nine occasions. When these incidents were investigated

> police found that in every case where the little girls had told their parents what had happened, their stories had been dismissed as nightmares. How many other children over the years have suffered this kind of trauma, only to have their

experience dismissed as fantasy by parents too deaf and blind to hear?[5]

2. Investigating child sexual abuse

a) Police

The police are charged with the prime responsibility for investigating the reported abuse with a view to obtaining evidence for a criminal conviction. What expectations do the police have in investigating child sexual abuse? A statement from a child is insufficient. Some other evidence is needed. Moreover, the guidance resulting from Lord Clyde's report and enacted in the Children Act is that children must be taken seriously but not necessarily believed. How does it feel not to be believed? Does it feel that you have been taken seriously?

The criminal justice system is based on the premise that evidence needs to be produced so that the prosecution case can be proved beyond reasonable doubt. The fact that abuse is taking place is not the point. The issue is whether in the investigation there is going to be enough evidence found to justify a conviction.

A member of one Woman and Child Unit advised me that over seventy-five per cent of investigations did not lead to charges being brought. In those that resulted in prosecution, two factors were important. There was corroboration; or there was an admission.

Corroboration is rare. There are either no witnesses, or there are witnesses who are at least implicated. Physical or medical evidence – a major factor in the Cleveland cases – can be corroboration, but that presupposes the nature of the sexual abuse. By no means all sexual abuse leaves *physical* evidence.

An admission of culpability is usually motivated by a

desire to change, and to receive help to change. It actually results in prosecution, the essential basis for the investigation, which is neither an inducement for adults to disclose their abuse of children nor indeed the way to ensure help to change is offered.

Children are often scared of the police, and my experience does not suggest that the introduction of non-uniformed, younger and female police officers has made a significant impact on how the police are perceived by children. They are still the police, and strangers, and can reputedly do awful things (like locking people away for being bad).

b) Social workers

Social workers often accompany the police during the investigations. Such joint working is now confirmed as good practice. The remit of social workers is to ensure the protection of the child, albeit this is belated (in that an investigation has resulted because of abuse being reported). There is a responsibility to produce evidence either to ensure that the child is now adequately protected or to support the contention that the child is still at risk of abuse.

The continuing presence of the alleged abusers in the house can in some cases be sufficient initial evidence. In this case the child can be compulsorily removed to a place of safety unless the alleged abusers agree voluntarily to stay elsewhere, or – under the Children Act – are legally excluded from the house, and have access to the child only in the company of another, presumed non-abusing, adult. The perception of social workers is not necessarily less fearsome than that of the police, as social workers can reputedly lock children away.

c) The child

A child may have reported something of an abusive nature to an adult, in the hope that some support or change might result. The child may have 'tested the water' with a small disclosure, to check whether it was safe to tell more, and then be completely confused and alarmed by the subsequent presence of the investigating officers.

The nature of the investigation, to produce evidence, is interrogatory and invasive. For a child it can be very difficult to be pinned into a particular form of disclosure. That is, a child may already feel confusion, unhappiness, fear, embarrassment and anxiety. Added to this is now concern and perhaps alarm at the presence of two new adults, often a policewoman and a social worker. It is neither easy nor necessarily appropriate for a child to frame those feelings into a 'who did what, where, how and when'. There is often a sense of shame and guilt that what has been reported has led to this investigation, and great fears regarding the consequences of reporting it to a policewoman and a social worker.

It must be remembered that the motive of children who report abuse is not to have an investigation launched.

3. Protecting children from sexual abuse

a) Understanding the risks

A child is potentially more at risk of abuse if the abuse has been reported and investigated and no further action taken. The abuse of power, upon which all abuse is founded, has not been arrested. Punishment, in the form of continued abuse, or the introduction of new forms of abuse or further abusers, can easily result.

Moreover, the time during which an investigation is

taking place, or (if the investigation has led to charges being brought) the months during which a trial is awaited, is a crucial period of risk for a child. But the alleged abuser is innocent until proven guilty. Until guilt is established – and even after it has been, for abusers do not necessarily become incarcerated – the child can easily remain at risk.

Moreover, it is not uncommon for courts to order unsupervised access, including residential access, to adults against whom abuse has been alleged by the child but against whom there has as yet been no criminal proceedings. This may be particularly true of allegations of sexual abuse perpetrated by women.

But other risks have been taken by the child who has reported abuse. The main risk is the deprivation of love and care by the adults against whom the abuse has been alleged. It must be understood that children see abusers as more than the abuse they perpetrate. These adults are fundamental in their lives. Therefore, disclosing abuse can make matters considerably more precarious for a child, not just in terms of further sexual abuse, but in terms of being loved at all.

It is rare for abusers to be unimportant and insignificant adults. They are often the most important adults for the abused children. Children do not need to be abused, but they do need those very adults who commit the abuse. The costs of disclosure may be the removal, physically, of these adults, or of the child from the adults. There may also be the withdrawal of emotional attachment, already distorted and vulnerable, by the adults.

A child who already senses that the abusing adults do not provide the appropriate love or care may well cling to what passes for it. Being protected equates with becoming further detached from any chance that the love so craved for will be given.

b) Shutting the stable door

Retrospective child protection – that is, offering protection after the damage has been done – is unlikely to feel convincing to a child. This is not just in a physical sense, in that a geographical distance is retained between abuser and abused. The child's experience of abuse is often that the abuser is omnipotent and omnipresent. Lying awake at night, terrified that the abuser will appear through the wall or out of the wardrobe or in the window does not feel like protection to the child.

In this sense the powers to exclude an alleged abuser from the house may have minimal benefits for the child. Although it is important that there is no further sexual abuse perpetrated, the child will not be free from the perceived power of the abuser solely by his or her removal.

c) The failure of protection from child sexual abuse

It is an absolute fallacy that the agencies charged with child protection (in particular social work) can actually protect a child from any particular abuser, or from being abused by other adults. This is as true for children currently unknown to the various agencies as it is for those who have already disclosed abuse.

Moreover, this is enshrined in law through the rights of parents to bring up their children in accordance with their wishes. It requires considerable evidence to remove these rights. Children have virtually no say in how they are parented, and even the explicit confirmation of the right of a child to express a view (and the presumption that a child over twelve years of age has a view) does not mean it will be followed, or even that a child would, in an abusive situation, feel empowered to express a view in contradiction to that of the abusers.

4. Prosecuting the perpetrators of child sexual abuse

a) The evidence

There is rarely significant and conclusive physical evidence of child sexual abuse. In situations where evidence corroborating some forms of child sexual abuse does exist it may be challenged, particularly if it indicates widespread abuse which has led to a public reaction against such allegations on a number of occasions (as it was in the cases in Cleveland).

b) The examination process

The credibility of those giving evidence is often challenged under cross-examination, and a practice of destroying the reputation of the witness has developed into an art. The focus is thus less on what happened but on making the witness appear incredible (however valid the evidence would otherwise be).

The difficulty experienced by children in giving evidence has only been marginally helped by the introduction of video links and screens. In every application for the use of these aids it has to be shown conclusively that they are essential to the child's ability to give evidence. They are not by any means automatically provided. A child may struggle to convey the evidence in a form that makes sense to the court or which can provide the index of certainty required.

Moreover, it is still a fundamental expectation that the witnesses identify their abuser in court. A number of supposedly watertight cases have failed because this simple task was too much for the witnesses.

c) The element of time

Court cases often take a year to begin. This is a very long time to wait in an adult's life – and considerably more so in a child's. The stress of this period is a significant destructive force for a child. Further, the importance placed on avoiding the contamination of evidence has been used either to prevent a child receiving therapy during this period – at a time when the child's recovery may well be in the balance – or to argue that the case cannot continue as the child's evidence is now circumspect due to the involvement of the child with a therapist.

5. Sentencing the convicted abusers

a) The provision of help

There is no obligation to provide therapy for abusers either in the community or in prison. Very few resources are available to offer long-term, skilled help to abusers (although there is now an increasing awareness and interest in this work among professionals). Nor is there an obligation generally placed on abusers to make use of any help that is available (unless they are placed on probation with a specific condition of treatment).

b) The principle of punishment

There is a fundamental problem with the underlying principle of the criminal justice system, and that is the concept of punishment. Punishment of an abuser is unlikely to provide any assistance for the abused child (other than physical separation). Indeed, the sense of guilt carried by children whose abusers are imprisoned can be enormous. Further, the fears that arise when the 'monster' is released can be totally disabling. Moreover, punishment is a great deterrent for abusers to admit and acknowledge their actions, with disastrous consequences in terms of the likelihood of an abuser reoffending and the abused children having to cope with a denial of their reality. I will return to this point later.

While there may be a widespread acceptance that the criminal justice system produces a slim chance of abusers being convicted, it is interesting that there is still a commitment to that system. This is not untypical of an informed position. After stating that professional systems are essential, a Childline/Community Care publication acknowledges the limitations of external controls and retrospective action:

> Try as the professionals do to build ever tighter sets of policies and procedures, they find that children are still assaulted. Indeed, it could be argued that the quest for increasingly legalistic solutions has left some children more exposed to abuse, and less accessible to help.[6]

Recent research in England argues that it is possible to increase the rate of conviction, but only 'because a realistic approach has been adopted when selecting which cases should be prosecuted . . . Serious contact abuse was the barometer most used by police when deciding whether to intervene, and the research also found more people pleaded guilty if the severity of the charge was reduced'.[7]

The logic of selecting out many cases, as not abusive enough or unrealistic to prosecute, and the minimisation of the offence, does nothing to inspire confidence in the criminal justice system as a method of protecting children from abuse.

Thus, I find it simple to summarise the impact of the criminal justice system on sexually abused children. It is abusive. It is *not about children*. It is experienced by them generally as destructive and punitive *of them*. Indeed, it would be hard to conceive of a process which from start to finish could be more designed not to serve an abused child's interests. It certainly does not place their welfare as paramount. Quite fundamentally it is an integral part of the abusive cycle which creates the conditions under which child sexual abuse can flourish. The cycle of abuse – the drama of the different roles that I identified in Chapter 3 – is consolidated and perpetuated by the criminal justice system. It is based on distorted thinking and distorted beliefs (such as a young child has the ability, in terms of knowledge, experience and motivation to make up stories about being abused). To the extent that we endorse or collude with the criminal justice system and its treatment of abused children we too are implicated in the abuse. We share their abusers' complicity.

It is not what we as Christians want for our children. We need to promote a kind of society and a morality which does not turn its back on sexually abused children or condemn them to further abuse – system abuse. If that means we need to remove the needs of children from the criminal justice system then so be it.

I will pick up this theme in later chapters, and indicate how we can address the needs of children and parents, teachers and other adults, within an ethical framework which is freed from the destructive powers of the current legal system. But first I wish to consider the climate of fear that has arisen in respect of children. Are we so concerned about our own safety, protecting our own innocence, that the sexual abuse of children is not our priority?

CHAPTER 5

FEARS AND ANXIETIES – THE PROBLEM FOR ADULTS

My questions

Are we afraid of children?
Do we fear that if a child discloses we could not cope?
Do we worry that a child will wrongly accuse us of abuse?
Are our motives or practices in being with children shameful?
Do we no longer know how to relate positively to children?
Have we lost our ability or confidence to show our love for our children?

'Don't touch'.

This edict might have been more commonly appended to fragile china or sophisticated technology. But the last decade has seen this label applied to children. I am not alluding to the kind of touch which has rightly been condemned – the traditional methods of physical chastisement. Rather, we are in a climate where, particularly within education, the injunction is not to touch children at all.

In Britain the introduction of Childline, the free telephone line that allows children to talk in confidence to an adult about their concerns, combined with the publicity and awareness arising from the media reporting of child abuse cases, and also the adoption of the Children Act, has coincided with a continual rise in allegations made by pupils against school teachers. As considerably less than ten per cent of these allegations have led to convictions, albeit not dissimilar to the rate of conviction in relation to all allegations of child sexual abuse, it is claimed that these may include a significant number of malicious accusations, which can have a devastating effect on a teacher's career and personal life. This was a point emphasised in 1995 at a major child protection conference by Ronnie Smith, general secretary of the Educational Institute of Scotland, who feared the lives of many dedicated and caring teachers were being ruined by unsubstantiated allegations of abuse by pupils.

The National Union of Schoolmasters and Union of Women Teachers has issued recommendations that teachers should as far as possible avoid all physical contact with pupils, including holding back from comforting them. Also, the Association of Head Teachers in Scotland has recommended that teachers should never be alone with a child, and certainly not in a closed room. This is to avoid what the AHTS regards as mischievous allegations, noting that too many children tell lies, and that 'even a three-year-old can unwittingly cause a great deal of difficulty for a school, its community and members of staff'.[1]

This has become the norm in most local authority and voluntary sector settings, not just in schools. For example, residential units for children and adolescents generally have clear guidelines on physical contact and physical restraint. Teachers and residential social workers have had to rethink their spontaneous approach to child care.

The emphasis has shifted from child protection to protection of adults from false allegations by children.

Parents, too, are not immune from this. The Children (Scotland) Act has given children the right to sue their parents for failure to fulfil their parental responsibilities. Although it can reasonably be assumed that litigation will be an infrequent feature of court time, it is nevertheless seen as a legitimate response. It is a concept borrowed from the United States of America, where human loss and injury in most contexts now has a monetary value, and where the adversarial system of justice is the frequently used and socially acceptable route to resolution.

Fear and anxiety around children has increased dramatically for teachers, residential social workers and care staff, youth club leaders, church youth leaders and parents. This is a major problem for adults, and I believe there are a number of consequences.

First, the message to children is that 'hugging', which I use as a generic term for appropriate physical demonstration of affection, care and concern, is a suspicious activity. Rather than an action that may be open to misinterpretation, it has become more clearly understood as essentially inappropriate and at least implicitly abusive, particularly if engaged in by males. The notion of private physical space has been highlighted to such an extent that it may now have created an atmosphere where there is considerable pressure for each child (and each adult) to be a physical and emotional island.

Secondly, a major form of expression has become taboo. Communication analysts suggest that at least ninety per cent of the communications we give and receive are non-verbal. Although we use millions of words to convey messages, meaning is transmitted and received to a much greater extent by the non-verbal communications

– for example, facial expressions, eye contact, body posture, physical touch. We are now having to verbalise the non-verbal, or (more likely) not communicating what we intend, and by this transmit to children our anxiety about being in their presence.

Thirdly, the lack of physical touch can breed detachment, by adults and children. Adults cope with their fears and anxieties by becoming emotionally distant. Children learn that physical affection from adult to child is either not appropriate or at least not required, and certainly not comfortable. These children learn how to be adults from their adult caretakers, and a longer-term consequence may be the increased detachment between parents and children in the next generation.

Fourthly, the notions of individual detachment and emotional independence are arguably peculiarly Western, and not unrelated to the kind of rational, scientific, technological, compartmentalised society we have created. We have our own work-space, our own computer, our own bedroom, and in some instances our own separate mealtimes apart from other family members. It is, then, relevant to see our response to our fears and anxieties about child care and child abuse as part of our more general pattern of relating to each other and to our world in Western society. We have become detached and self-contained, independent of each other except through artificial and technological communications. We may see each other not as people but as fellow operatives.

One of the responses to these fears has been to debate the need for a 'hugger's charter' for professionals working with children,[2] which would give specific guidance on what to do (or not do) and when to do it. It is another example of the way child care and child protection has become institutionalised through guide-lines in an attempt to produce standardised formulas to meet the needs of adults. As was made clear in the previous chapter, this is far less about children and far more about adults' needs: the need to cover your back, to be beyond reproach, to be able to hold up a folder of guidance and affirm that it was followed to the letter. *Mea non culpa*.

The problem for adults relating to children of whom they are not the parents is compounded by the legacy of the 'stranger-danger' alarms. The belief that children are at risk of abuse from (male) strangers, fed by dramatic, terrifying but isolated instances of such abuse, creates a fear of wrongful accusation among adults. They must ensure that they are not open to accusations of being a 'beast' or a 'monster', that their innocent intentions have not been horrifically misconstrued and that they will be forever tainted with suspicion. The fact that abuse is overwhelmingly more prevalent within the home, perpetrated by parents and other trusted adult or adolescent caretakers, seems not to deflect from this fear. For instance, Childline Scotland reports that only eight per cent of calls allege sexual abuse by a stranger, and that figure is likely to be far greater than the actual percentage as it is accepted it is harder to report abuse being inflicted within the home.

This has led to the increased use by parents of controlled, supervised settings for their children, such as nurseries, after-school clubs, youth clubs and activity camps, rather than allowing them to play unsupervised. Or keeping them indoors or within the home environment. As Quigley writes in *Scotland on Sunday*, there is

a climate of fear that permeates the thoughts of every parent in Britain . . . Only three per cent of those questioned thought children were very safe when they were away from their homes or families, either out playing or at school. In their efforts to keep them safe, however, parents are in danger of depriving their children of their childhood. Children no longer play freely outside in the summer until darkness falls. A generation of children is growing up unable to mix easily with others, make decisions or take risks.

Children are living increasingly restricted lives as parents try and do what is right and keep them safe from three all-consuming worries: paedophiles, traffic and bullies.[3]

These organised child-care settings are less likely to attract men to them, as a recent report[4] has identified that the perception of men, rather than women, as potential pae-dophiles is ensuring the child-care profession remains overwhelmingly female. Indeed, men rather than women are acutely worried about the risk of being accused of child abuse. The reaction to men who show interest in working in child care ranges from considering them to be somewhat strange to viewing them with suspicion, as a significant potential risk to children. This is despite societal moves towards equal opportunities.

The impact of these implicit messages on children is abusive. The messages relay that 'if you are a boy, you may grow up to contain evil that makes you a dangerous stranger to children; and if you are a girl, you must always be alert to the danger presented by strange men. That is the reason we have banished men from the nursery – because they are not safe and cannot be trusted. That is why men are not allowed to smile at you, speak to you, touch you. Women, however, are safe, and can be trusted.' And so we perpetuate the cycle of abuse within the collective psyche.

There are two other, and perhaps more fundamental, aspects to the adult fear of children. The first is the concept that children are actually the legal property of their parents. While the possibility of litigation by children against their parents for failing to meet their parental responsibilities is now enacted, the prospect of which has induced some alarm among parents, it is a different fear that still predominates. This is the fear of the reactions by the children's owners should an adult who is not the parent dare to intervene in that parent's child care or directly with the child.

An illustration of this starkly hit the world through the abduction and murder by two young boys of two-year-old James Bulger in Bootle, England, in February 1993. The cruelty of the boys who committed the murder, apparently calculated, and certainly pursued to its conclusion over a period of hours, was not the only alarming feature. Indeed, for Helen Dunmore, the children's novelist,

> the most disturbing aspect of the Bulger case was not the actions of the two ten-year-olds, but the inaction of the adults who saw James being abducted and did nothing about it. When children are seen as private property there's no community responsibility for their welfare.[5]

Adults are scared of intervening – interfering – with other people's children. They have no rights over these children so they assume no responsibility. As the Children Act in Britain enshrines rights and responsibilities in parents, unless there is an order removing them, this leaves no role for other adults. This is a crucial area that I will consider again later.

The second most important aspect of the adult fear of children is based on the confusion about what is expected of children. For contrary to what we might assume, childhood as a concept has not always existed – in medieval times it seems there was no such thing as childhood – and its nature has changed over the centuries. The first images of childhood were angelic, particularly featuring the infant Jesus, and progressing to the naked child, the epitomy of asexual human innocence and holiness.[6] This evolved into the idea of the child as an empty vessel to be filled with adult knowledge – to be schooled. However, the move into the industrial period reframed children as economic burdens until they could be invested as wage-earning labourers, the property of their adult caretakers. They were mini-adults, and often portrayed as such.

In this century children have become more of an emotional than economic investment. Adults seeking their emotional nurturance through their children is no less destructive than exploiting their physical labour for money. However, the reliance on children to do this requires compliance and dependence. Children who have rights, for example of opinions and expression of their views, of how they are brought up, and whether or not they accept medical treatment, yet who at the same time are financially dependent for a substantial number of years – well beyond the school-leaving age in many cases – present a threat to their parents. Recent civil court cases in Britain of adult students suing their parents for financial support to undertake their studies at university underlines this.

The reactions to this threat include two particularly pernicious and unhealthy responses, both driven by fear. First, there is enforced power for the children to 'pay their way' by meeting the adults' emotional needs. Adults may fear they will be abandoned emotionally by their children, and become abusive in their demands. They may also be ensuring that the children know their place, that the adults who bore them and feed them have rights of possession and rights to a pay-back. Indeed, the motivation to have children may be driven by this need. From this follows the scope for mothers not to separate themselves from their children, and to see them as extensions of themselves to be used to meet their emotional and physical needs.

Secondly, there is detachment, a delegation to children to bring themselves up while the adults get on with their own lives. This is the fear that the children are a drain on them, that they will be demanding of them in emotional terms as well as economic. The children are paid off financially – 'here's some money to go out', 'here's a computer to play with in your room' – and materialistic child care prevails.

This is an illustration of how some of the elements of fear and detachment can combine. A recent late evening curfew on children being outdoors without good reason has been introduced in part of the town of Hamilton, in South Lanarkshire, Scotland, and it is suggested this type of social control of children may extend to other communities. The justification for this curfew in Hamilton seems to be twofold. First, there are those who highlight that children in this area – which comprises overwhelmingly public sector housing where indices of poverty are well represented, and which is known locally as The Jungle and Wine Alley – are frequently involved in offending, and that this curfew is required for the public to be safe from children. Some opponents of this curfew see it as a case of 'blaming the victims' of poverty rather than addressing the causes.

On the other hand, there is an argument that the curfew is the result of parents being unable or unwilling to curb their children's behaviour. Some of the consequences of children being out late at night include disruption within schools the following day, tiredness and health problems.

The issue for proponents of this argument in favour of the curfew is that children are being neglected, under-parented, and that there is a degree of indifference by the parents to what their children are doing.

At the same time, some parents in Hamilton whose children are affected by this curfew are unwilling to acknowledge the right of anyone else, whether other adults or public authorities, to determine what they should or should not be allowed to decide in terms of their children's welfare. A Glasgow head teacher, Maire Whitehead, welcomes the curfew

> because it will force parents to face the reality of their children's lifestyle and help curb tiredness and drunkenness among children. All these factors have an impact on children in school. The parents are too tired themselves and just want a bit of peace, so they aren't going to ask too many questions. It is neglect rather than cruelty. They are not giving their children their time. They are only too willing to believe where their children say they're going, because it suits the image they want to have of them.[7]

Both emotional dependency – which can include shaping children into the parents' desired image of what they, the parents, need their children to be – and emotional detachment, within a basis of power whereby adults still have possession of children, and rights and responsibilities over their children to the exclusion of other adults, creates the climate for widespread abuse.

This is compounded by our mixed messages regarding children's sexuality. The age of consent to sexual acts has not always been sixteen years, as it currently is in Britain. It was as low as ten years, and has risen over the centuries. Thus, some instances of what we would now classify as sexual abuse would have been socially, legally (and morally) accepted. Even though we still express notions of children being (sexually) innocent, children are acknowledged to have sexual arousal, even as infants, and it seems we increasingly promote this aspect of their personality by the way we clothe our children as miniature adults, in the same adult fashions that often contain sexual messages and images. We promote the Lolita syndrome.

It is not unusual for an abuser to develop distorted thinking and beliefs which attribute to the victim the role of seducer. But do we contribute to that distortion by the way we encourage our children to dress and to act, and by their exposure to adult role models and images that are explicitly sexual? The current obvious example of this might be the media-induced pre-pubescent zeal for the Spice Girls, whose 'girl-power' is quite explicitly sexual. If this is the message we want to convey to both boys and girls, then what are we doing to ensure that their response is not going to exacerbate the risks of them being sexually abused? Parents may see their young children as sexual beings in a physical sense, but this is way beyond children's emotional and social comprehension, and their self-perception. Parents may not realise how this affects their children by confusing their image and exposing them to potential abuse.

While in the West we may publicly protest that children should retain their sexual innocence, a lucrative trade in young children for sexual tourists from the Western world is still being exploited in some south-east Asian countries. Our actions do not coincide with our words. We must question to what extent we are setting children up to fail, to blame themselves for their victimisation, to carry the responsibility for their abuse because of the way they acted or dressed.

Our confusion about what childhood means has left us giving ambiguous messages to children. It has left them confused. It has left us deskilled and we feel exposed to blame if we 'get it wrong', particularly with other people's children. The problem for adults is fear. Fear eats the soul. The current climate of child care is essentially soulless. It is clinical and detached – the 'don't touch' model, or it is dominating, demanding and exploitative. These are the two ends of the same continuum of fear. If we live in a climate where we are unclear about why we have children, what we expect of them, what their relationship to their parents and other adult caretakers is or should be, and what place they have in society, we convey the message that we distrust them. Our distrust and fear leaves them open to abuse, and closes our ears to what they might tell us. Beatrix Campbell states that 'a society in which adults are estranged from the world of children, and often from their own childhood, tends to hear children's speech only as a foreign language, or as a lie'.[8]

Adults have become bystanders to children's experiences. In my work with children on bullying, it is absolutely clear that children have a very extensive and sophisticated understanding of what is happening between them in their relationships, and the parts that adults play which perpetuate the bullying cycle. In one exercise (which I have entitled the blame – no responsibility matrix) children are astute in identifying all the ways in which adults who choose to investigate (using the blame-punishment-rescue response) are fobbed off with denials of knowledge and responsibility.[9] These include:

'I wasn't there'   'Who? Me?'   'It wasn't me'
'It was him/her/them'   'I saw nothing'
'Why are you picking on me?'   'It was just a game'

'Bullying? What bullying?'
And the ubiquitous 'I don't know'.

Children are adept at knowing when to see no evil, hear no evil and speak no evil. Adults will only make the situation worse. And, of course, many adults know they are only playing the game too. They want to be *seen* to be taking the matter seriously, rather than actually taking responsibility for achieving a resolution of what are generally extremely complex relationship difficulties.

In the context of child sexual abuse these bystander patterns illustrate the survival strategies adopted by adults whose fear prevents them from coping with their actual complicity in what is taking place, and seeking positive resolutions which protect and support children. Clarkson has distinguished a dozen variations of the bystander role which I have slightly adapted.[10] These are:

It's none of my business (like Pontius Pilate, I'm washing my hands of it).

I want to keep out of it, not take sides, be neutral.

The truth lies somewhere in between (they're both equally to blame).

I don't want to rock the boat and be seen to cause trouble.

It's more complex than it seems, it's all too difficult for me to get involved.

I don't understand all that's going on, I don't have the information (and I don't want it either).

I don't want to get burned again, which is what happened the last time I tried to do something.

I can't do anything about it on my own, it's all too big.

I'm only telling the truth as I see it ('gossip is juicier than responsibility').

I'm only following orders/guidelines/just doing my job.

I'm keeping my own counsel, it's not my problem.

The victim brought it on herself/himself/themselves.

We have sophisticated patterns of behaviour which are our adaptive responses to fear. These lead us to adopt roles which form a cycle of abuse, either actively within the roles of persecutor, victim, rescuer, indifferent, punisher, or the peripheral, inactive – but fundamental – bystander. My examination of the relationships that we have chosen to develop with each other, and in particular with children, have raised more questions. I need to discover what kind of moral context can provide the climate and support for all of us to enable our children to be free from abuse, and to be really supported and truly helped when they are abused. I need to know whether Christianity can provide that moral context, or whether Christianity colludes with the climate of abuse. These questions are so critical to my argument that I will later examine the basis of my own faith in God, a faith that has been tested in the ultimate way – by having to cope as a parent with the horror that two of my children have been sexually abused.

But first, if we are confronted by the reality of a sexually abused child, how do we cope with our fears? How do we respond if a child does actually break through their survival strategy of silence? How do we allow children to break through our survival strategies as bystanders, or through our roles in the cycle of abuse, and tell us they have suffered sexual abuse?

What do we do when the sexually abused child is right in front of us?

CHAPTER 6

COPING WITH DISCLOSURES

My questions

Why do children disclose?
What does it feel like to disclose?
What happens to children who disclose?
Does telling lead to healing?
What does it feel like to listen to a child disclose sexual abuse?
Can a child's disclosure be abusive to the adults hearing it?
How do non-abusing parents cope with their children's disclosures?

Children do disclose abuse: they do speak the unspeakable.

When I was being abused I felt so alone, dirty and guilty. When I finally got the courage to tell and was met with disbelief, I still felt alone, dirty and guilty. If someone says they are being abused, professionals, family and friends must listen, hear and support the survivor.[1]

This young woman, whose life was portrayed in a Meridian

TV drama documentary entitled *No Child of Mine*, first shown in Britain in February 1997, was sexually abused by her mother and step-father from the age of ten years, was subsequently hired out for sex, was taken into care and raped by a residential care worker, and then used by a pimp.

As Miles notes,

> even when undeniable evidence of abuse is laid at the door of respected figures like headmasters or priests, the first reflex of the authorities is almost always to close ranks behind the abuser and cover his tracks. Case after case shows colleagues, bosses and official bodies instinctively bending the truth or deliberately lying in order to protect the offender rather than do justice to the victim.[2]

Child prostitution, a familiar feature in Asian tourist resorts, is prevalent in Britain, and The Children's Society has reported that 4,000 girls, some as young as ten years of age, were cautioned by the police for soliciting between 1989 and 1995. These figures are seen as the tip of the iceberg.[3] An employee of The Children's Society, Penny Dean, concludes:

> We know that these children have fallen through every safety net there is. Many have been abused or neglected as young children, and experience disrupted and unsettled lives which leave them vulnerable to adults who target them for abuse. If there is one common denominator, it is that these children and young people simply do not feel anybody cares about them. As a result, they don't feel they matter.[4]

It seems to me we have reached the fundamental basis not just of why children don't tell, but what they need from adults in order that they can tell.

Children need to know that they matter. But even that is not enough. Children are astute. They know when they have to keep their secrets, they can sense when an adult cannot hear them, cannot cope with the pain, cannot protect them from the consequences of telling. Even children regarded as 'stupid', those who are classified as 'mentally handicapped' or with 'learning difficulties', can know if and when the adults around them can and cannot cope with being exposed to the child's pain beneath the smile.[5]

One of the fears currently prevalent in education is that a child will disclose abuse to a teacher, who is likely to feel unskilled, dysfunctional and disabled by this. Local authority guide-lines, which direct the ways in which schools can process a child who discloses (or who is suspected to have suffered) abuse, may provide some support. At least there is someone else who can be called on to deal with it. But of course life is rarely as simple as that, and for the teacher who is presented with a child who may be experiencing abuse, panic can set in.

The more likely scenario, which contributes to the low incidence of disclosure, is that the implicit message is expressed as loud and clear from schools as the (generally explicit) message from the abusers: 'don't tell'. Or, in an individual teacher's case, 'don't tell me'. The defences put forward by teachers are understandable. They are not trained to handle disclosures; they may make a mess of it; they may contaminate evidence; they won't know what to say or how to react; they may get interrupted; the environment is not conducive (they aren't supposed to be in a closed room alone with a child); it will take time which they don't have to give. And it isn't their job. Their job is to teach children, not get involved in child protection or child abuse.

Teachers are not alone. No one else particularly wants to hear about it either. Why would they? The emotional impact on an adult who has been trusted by the child, and who has listened to that child recount experiences of being sexually abused by an adult, is tremendous. It is always traumatic. Often the abuser is known to this adult, which makes this harder still, and can compound issues of loyalty. The disclosure of abuse may also raise a number of unresolved issues of their own for the adults to whom the child talks.

There are further ramifications of being the adult to whom the child discloses. There is the prospect of being called as a witness in any court case arising from these allegations. There is the role that the child has put the adult in, of being trusted with this information which in itself can be life-threatening for the child, and which may be a burden that the adult finds unbearable. There is also the implicit expectation that the adult can make the situation better for the child, which may well not be possible. The consequences of failing the expectations of the abused child can be enormously hard to bear.

A child who chooses an adult to tell has made a powerful claim on that adult. And that may be well beyond the call of duty, as determined in the job description.

Although much of the material is applicable to all adults who hear a child's disclosure of sexual abuse, I want to focus for a while on a particular adult-child relationship, that of the non-abusing parent. What does it feel like, for example, for a non-abusing parent to hear that their child has been sexually abused by their other parent? And what does it feel like if their children talk directly to them about their experiences of sexual abuse perpetrated by their other parent?

Perhaps this question would be just as powerful left unanswered by me, so that the readers who have children can spend time considering the impact this would have on them. But I will attempt to convey some of the reactions that non-abusing parents do experience, by placing the impact of a child's disclosure on the non-abusing parent in the context of currently accepted guide-lines of good practice in working with (adult) survivors of child sexual abuse.[6]

1. Believe survivors – children rarely make up stories of abuse

The immediate reaction of a non-abusing parent is often total disbelief. What the child is telling is incomprehensible. This reaction is not confined to non-abusing parents. After my daughter told an experienced female detective constable about the abuse she had suffered, the police-woman came into our kitchen visibly pale, grasped the back of a chair for support, and said, in a state of shock, 'It obviously happened. Do you think it is true?'

Disbelief is a common response. Abuse doesn't fit in with preconceived assumptions about the way adults generally are with children, let alone your child and, where the abuser is the other parent, with assumptions about your partner. It attacks the core of the marital relationship; and of the relationship of the non-abusing parent to the child. It challenges the competence of the non-abusing parent even to know what was going on in the child's life, as well as the ability of the non-abusing parent to protect the child. Rather than offer unconditional acceptance of the child's story by believing it, the reaction is more likely to be a shocked and angry denial of what the child is saying. The non-abusing parent in effect may scream 'no' to the child. Given that the child may have adopted survival strategies including the suppression of memories of the abuse, the reaction of the non-abusing parent in denying the reality will compound the damage done to the child.

2. Acknowledge that the child has been damaged by the abuse

Given that it is so hard to acknowledge the child has actually been abused, it is a further more difficult and traumatic step for a non-abusing parent to accept that the child has been damaged by the abuse perpetrated by the other parent. The strong desire is for it all to be a bad dream, and for it all to be over and better. The non-abusing parent may crave for the safe, child-like notion of happy families.

3. Be explicit that it is not the child's fault or responsibility

There is a very real danger that the messenger gets shot: the child is blamed either for making up terrible lies, dirty and disgusting stories, or for bringing the abuse on themselves. 'Blame the victim.' This is a defence against the non-abusing parent's fears of complicity: how did I not know what was going on? Have I neglected my child? Am I at fault? How have I allowed such horrors to happen to my child?

4. Be aware of what the child may be going through in trying to heal

Telling is the start of healing, but it is only the very beginning. Being believed is a vital component in the healing process; it is the basis of re-establishing trust that has so severely been betrayed. Yet the consequence for non-abusing parents is the realisation that the trust placed by them in their partners has been betrayed. The acceptance of the child's abuse, the damage done to them, the destruction of their childhood, is the acceptance that the non-abusing parent's world can no longer be the same – the parental and family experiences are overturned. The abuse experienced by the non-abusing parent in this situation can be overwhelming, with major implications for their own healing. For the non-abusing parent has been fundamentally betrayed too.

5. Don't sympathise with the abuser

The non-abusing parent is often caught between loyalty to the child and loyalty to the abusing parent. The sense of confusion for the non-abusing parent mirrors the confusion experienced by the abused child. Thoughts, emotions, beliefs are in a turmoil.

6. Recognise that the child may have confused feelings about the abuser

The emotional turmoil for the child, while it can be mirrored by the non-abusing parent, can be problematic too. For at the point when the non-abusing parent is able to believe what has happened to the child, is able to acknowledge the damage done, can understand the enormity of the healing process ahead for the child, and can place the responsibility fairly and squarely on the abuser and not on the child – this is the time that the non-abusing parent may want to murder the abuser. Recognising that the child may have some strong emotional attachment to the abusing parent is not good news for the non-abusing parent, and can set off a chain of thoughts and actions which attempt to consolidate within the child the non-abusing parent's own hatred of the abuser.

7. Acknowledge the child's fear, anger, pain and confusion

It is never easy to cope with and support a child's emotions of deep hurt or terror. The child's pain hurts the parent too. It can be extremely hard for a non-abusing parent to support and comfort a child experiencing such emotions when the cause of these emotions has been the abuse inflicted by the other parent. Although separating out what the non-abusing parent feels (about the abuse and the abuser) from what the child feels is crucial, emotions can easily become confused. Moreover, the child will look to the non-abusing parent as a guide: is it legitimate to feel all these emotions?

8. Express your compassion

One of the most important expressions of emotion required from the non-abusing parent is compassion for the child. Whatever else is happening inside, the indisputable and unconditional care, concern and empathy for what the child has undergone is vital. At a time when the non-abusing parent may need much support, comfort and reassurance, there is sometimes too little left to give to the child.

9. Respect the time, space and process of healing

Wanting the child to recover quickly is a natural response. But healing takes time, and takes many turns. This would in any event drain the resources of a non-abusing parent. However, much more is encountered: police and social work investigations, lawyers and prosecutors, court cases, as well as the responses of extended family members, friends and neighbours. As was illustrated earlier, the criminal justice approach to child protection is extremely harrowing and destructive for the child, but also for the non-abusing parent. The criminal justice system is not sensitive to the need for a child to heal, it wants to punish. Innocent or guilty, not whole and healthy, are its bywords. If the non-abusing parent is a father, then there is an even rougher ride experienced. I will reflect on this later.

10. Encourage the child to use other support as well as you

Although it is apparent that the burden of support for the child needs to be shared around, there is a major problem in knowing who could offer support and how that could be done. This is more than just establishing who might have the skills, knowledge and capacity to cope with what the child has experienced and offer appropriate support, however important these factors are. Trust has been betrayed, and that betrayal is experienced by both the child and the non-abusing parent. If the abuse has been perpetrated by a parent, the most logical person to support a child, and an adult on whom the child depended (and who may have been seen as God-like in importance), who can the child now trust?

If the non-abusing parent had been unaware of what the other parent was doing to their child, how can that parent now feel confident to use the support of other, and presumably less intimately known, adults?

11. Find support for yourself – the healing process will take its toll on you too

The non-abusing parent will experience trauma from hearing the child disclose abuse which itself requires time and support to heal. In effect the non-abusing parent experiences abuse. This can be compounded by the criminal justice system's handling of abuse allegations, and it is not uncommon for both child and non-abusing parent to experience 'agency abuse'. Not only does the child's healing process take its toll on the non-abusing parent, who may generally be the prime person to help the child through that process, but the legacy of the abuse experienced by the non-abusing parent through the times of disclosure and the subsequent investigations takes its toll. The non-abusing parent will never be the same person again, even if the healing process is successful.

There is a sense of chronic sorrow: that the abuse happened, that the child could not have had the kind of childhood that any child deserves. There is chronic guilt and shame and sense of failure that the abuse happened, and that the non-abusing parent did not prevent it. The child was abandoned, albeit unwittingly, by the non-abusing parent. Part of the healing process may be for the child to express the legitimate anger at this parent – for not being there, for failing to protect the child. Elsewhere the parent can experience the societal fingers of blame: 'you must have known what was going on', 'what kind of parent are you?' The non-abusing parent carries the stigma, the betrayal, the powerlessness and the traumatic sexualisation (often in terms of not wanting anything more to do with sexual relationships with the opposite sex) in the same way as the sexually abused child. Finding a network of supportive adults, who can actually extend themselves to offer care and compassion to the non-abusing parent, can be extremely difficult. Many other adults appear to just not want to know.

12. Appreciate that your relationship with the child may need to develop over time

It is easy for a non-abusing parent and child to become stuck in their relationship. It may be that the reaction to the abuse has left the non-abusing parent less able to express physical affection to the child – a form of the 'don't touch' syndrome mentioned earlier. This can itself be hard for the child, and be experienced as a sense of rejection and a confirmation of the stigma borne. There will be layers of different emotions for both parties in this relationship, and many aspects of not only the abuse but also the role of the non-abusing parent may need to be explored, perhaps a number of times. A closeness in the relationship between child and non-abusing parent may be assumed because the child has taken the risk to disclose, and because the non-abusing parent has expressed the belief that it happened, has acknowledged the damage done and has shown compassion. But it is not that simple. There is tension in the relationship which survives, an inability to return to the state of innocence. Each by their presence reminds the other of what has happened. In time the relationship may only be able to develop through physical separation. Who wants to be reminded, day in and day out, of the suffering each has experienced?

13. See the child as a survivor, not a victim

The cycle of abuse contains victims and perpetrators, punishers and rescuers, the indifferent and the bystander. It is not only the abused child (the victim) who needs to be recast, reclassified. Indeed, for healing to take place the non-abusing parent has to help all those in relationship with the child to remove themselves from the roles within the cycle of abuse. The non-abusing parent will trap the child, themselves and others in the cycle if the roles remain but shift from person to person. Thus, if the non-abusing parent becomes the victim (for example, of abuse by the criminal justice system) or the punisher (of the abuser), then the cycle continues.

As I prepare to look at how we can break the cycle of abuse, create supportive networks for adults and parents, and establish non-abusive child care, I need to take stock of what all my questions have provided me with in terms of answers so far.

First, there is a great cause for a great many children to weep. There is evidence to suggest that the incidence of child sexual abuse is no less prevalent now than in the past, and retrospective studies of childhood sexual abuse remembered and reported indicate that as many as one in four children overall may be sexually abused by the age of eighteen years.[7]

Secondly, sexual abuse has a terrible impact on children, which often leads to significant long-term psychological damage. In order to survive, children adopt a range of survival strategies, most of which are designed to prevent their abuse being known.

Thirdly, child sexual abuse is not a random activity. It is overwhelmingly based within relationships where the abuser is in a trusted position of power and where the child is dependent, at least at times, on that person. Child sexual abuse is often located within a cycle of abuse where the adults and children fulfil destructive roles in relation to each other (such as victim, perpetrator, rescuer, punisher, indifferent and bystander). These roles are very common within many societal relationships, not just within families. Children are taught these roles, albeit implicitly, at a very early age.

Fourthly, child protection agencies and the criminal justice system could not cope with the extent of child sexual abuse, were it all to be reported. Indeed, there is an in-built resistance to the disclosure of sexual abuse by children, particularly where multiple and female abusers may be evident. Moreover, the criminal justice system is abusive itself – of children and of non-abusing parents – with its motivating purpose either to have concrete evidence of abuse to convict and punish an abuser or to conclude there is insufficient evidence to proceed, rather than help break through the cycle of abuse, prevent abuse and help the abused child to heal. The abusive aspects of the criminal justice system include: the impact on the child of not being believed, or of having to justify the allegation and, if the case gets that far, give evidence in court; the length of time it takes for the investigation and prosecution (if any) to be undertaken; the prevention of the child from receiving help to begin the healing process until the court case is dealt with (or dropped) for fear of contaminating evidence; the presumption of innocence of the abuser, and implicitly therefore the guilt or dishonesty of the child alleging abuse. Even if a conviction is likely, the use of plea-bargaining to reduce or minimise the offence, can also take place. All these aspects compound the child's feelings of powerlessness, betrayal and stigmatisation.

Fifthly, adults are fearful of children, unsure how to relate to them and what they expect of them. They fear that children will wrongly accuse them of sexual abuse, and further that children may have the motivation and power to destroy adult lives. They may encourage children to dress and behave in adult ways, as both a defence and confirmation that children are potential seducers: in effect, that children are sinful as much as (or more than) sinned against. It is a common adult response to use their fear as an excuse not to reach out to children who may be in desperate need of their care and compassion. They turn away, protect themselves and effectively become detached and indifferent to them. They fulfil the roles of indifferent or bystander in the cycle of abuse.

Sixthly, the burden on the child's caretaker, such as a non-abusing parent, is enormous. The process of helping a child to heal from their abuse presents fundamental issues for the non-abusing parent, even though that parent may be best placed through their relationship with the child to be the prime adult to do this. This is true of a step-parent, and even a foster parent too. Without a tremendous amount of care and compassion and support for this parent, the child will not be able to be helped to heal effectively. Those who care for a sexually abused child, or friends or relatives who are exposed to the knowledge of that abuse, become the secondary victims. Likewise those who care for or are a friend or relative of an abuser of children also become the secondary victims. The victimisation of the people who are in these roles is not necessarily a lesser form of what is experienced by the child on whom the sexual abuse has been perpetrated – it can be equally or more destructive. In families where one parent is the abuser of the children, the non-abusing parent is in the most dreadful situation. This can also apply to a non-abused sibling of an abused child. The betrayal of loyalties by the abusing parent, the internalised devastation of betrayal by the non-abusing parent or sibling of the child who was not protected, the feelings of inadequacy as a parent and a marital partner (or as an older brother or sister), let alone any victimisation that may result from a criminal investigation, leave this secondary victim truly damaged.

Finally, it cannot be stressed too strongly that everyone

within the cycle of abuse is damaged. All need to survive, but in ways that are wholesome and healthy. This is an arduous and often unsuccessful process, and is a focal point of this book. We do not create the conditions in society which allow people to heal, which allow people to break from unhealthy patterns, and which prevent the cycle of abuse being perpetuated. Not only do we refuse or fail to see and hear the distress of children, we fail to see other adults and children, secondary victims like the non-abusing parents and siblings, who despair too. By not hearing those who weep we condemn them to their misery. There are only two sides we can take; there is no neutral ground. 'Passivity in the face of evil from any vantage point is complicity with it.'[8]

By being open to listening we help. By not hearing we condemn.

So far I have made extensive use of the academic research and literature to help me answer my questions. Although I may be clearer about the issues than I was, there are a great many other issues presented that need to be addressed if we are to create a society where child sexual abuse does not need to exist, and where – as and when it does – we can all share in the responsibility to help the child heal and break out of the cycle of abuse. Despite the importance of the guidelines of good practice in helping adult survivors recover from their abuse, I have not found all the answers I need in my research so far. And maybe I won't find them in the usual literature.

I am left with some other questions, big questions, that need to be asked. And they need to be addressed not to any academic or researcher, nor to perpetrators or survivors, nor to carers of abused children. This time I want answers from God.

CHAPTER 7

THE FILTH AND THE FAITH – WHERE DOES GOD FIT IN?

My questions

If God exists why does he allow children to be sexually abused?
How is God experienced by a child who is sexually abused?
What is the impact on children if a church official abuses them?
What is the Church prepared to do about child sexual abuse?
How can children and non-abusing parents find faith after experiencing abuse?

There is a fundamental problem with evil within the Christian faith. The problem is this: if God exists, is omnipotent, omniscient and the perfection of goodness, how can evil exist? For God would understand the nature and prevalence of evil, would have the power to eliminate evil, and would have no limits on the power to intervene.[1] As my rector told me, he did not believe that any God that he could understand would want children to be sexually abused. The problem of evil is one that cannot be bypassed, and as I seek answers to my questions I will return to this central issue.

One of the ways to seek God's answers to my questions is to study his words, as written in the Bible, and even more so through the account of the teachings of Jesus in the Gospels. However, the Gospel of Matthew presents us with some fundamental difficulties when addressing the questions I have raised, particularly if we accept the Gospel literally, and without reference either to the context in which the teachings were conducted, or the social, historical and linguistic context in which the reputed author of the Gospels recorded them.[2] I have chosen this Gospel, for although it is now not commonly regarded as the earliest of the synoptic texts, nevertheless it contains all the essential elements of Mark (generally accepted as the primary Gospel) as well as other source material (commonly referred to as Q). I will refer particularly to chapters 5, 10 and 18 of Matthew's Gospel as I explore the issues of omnipotence, retribution and punishment, suffering and forgiveness.

Child sexual abuse is a fundamental violation of trust, a human betrayal. It also violates a child's ability to place trust in God, in a God of love and compassion, omnipotence and justice. Sexual abuse can be seen by the child as evidence that God does not exist, the experience of abuse contravening any meaningful notions of a caring, compassionate being who through Jesus emphasised that no one must harm children for fear of severe punishment (or at least dire consequences): 'If anyone causes one of these little ones who believe in me to sin, it would be better for him to have a millstone hung around his neck and to be drowned in the depths of the sea' (Matthew 18:6). However, the evidence of such dire consequences is rare. The vast majority of perpetrators are never investigated, let alone punished. The child may experience this as God's empty promises.

Alternatively, the child may see the sexual abuse as evidence that God does exist, and that the abuse is a punishment of the child by God, a divine retribution for real or imagined wrong doing. In other words, the child has the millstone hung round his or her neck and is drowned in the depths of the sea, a reasonably accurate account of how some survivors of abuse actually experience their lives. Thereby the child's concept of God becomes a variation of God as another abuser. The child may internalise a kind of heaven and hell reckoning or judgement along the lines of 'if you are good, I will not allow you to be abused, but if you are bad you will be punished'.

On the other hand, maybe God is not omnipotent. Maybe God cannot stop children being abused (albeit he has some powers to punish the abusers). 'Woe to the world because of the things that cause people to sin! Such things must come, but woe to the man through whom they come' (Matthew 18:7). But is God's vengeance meted out directly, or through the authorities of the state, or through the Church? We know that the criminal justice system fails dreadfully. We are unaware that God intervenes directly with abusers. That leaves us to consider the Church, God's representative body on earth.

Churches have been no more willing to acknowledge and respond to the issues of child sexual abuse than any other organisation. Indeed, given that churches are made up of ordinary mortals, it would be unlikely, if not unreasonable, that members of Christian congregations adopt a more enlightened and proactive role with regard to child sexual abuse than non-Christians. Moreover, there is both a darker side to the issue and a more complex one.

First, child sexual abuse is also perpetrated by priests and ministers of religion. Secondly, the Christian edict to forgive sinners leaves members of the congregations confused and uneasy in their role of supporting and protecting children from abusers. Thirdly, the Gospel message is that those who follow Christ will suffer persecution. I will look at each of these points in turn.

Three cases of substantial child sexual abuse have hit the Roman Catholic Church during 1997. Father Brendan Smyth was jailed for twelve years in Dublin, Ireland after admitting seventy-four offences of indecent assault and sexual abuse of males and females over a thirty-six year period to 1993. He had previously been sentenced in Northern Ireland to four years imprisonment in 1994 for sexually abusing children in Belfast over a twenty-year period. He also sexually abused an altar boy in North Dakota, in the United States of America, when he was posted there briefly.

Smyth is a member of the Nobertine Order. *The Guardian* reported the outcome of the court case, and the response from the Nobertine Order: 'The Order said it was now "painfully aware" of the inadequacy of its response over the years to reports of the priest's behaviour . . . Attempts to treat his deviancy were not only unsuccessful but also indicated that at least some people within his order may have known what he was up to.'[3]

In the same newspaper on the same day there was another account of child sexual abuse, this time in the United States of America. Although there had been no criminal proceedings instigated, a civil court case for damages had been brought by ten victims (and the family of an eleventh victim who had since committed suicide) against Rudolph Kos, a Roman Catholic priest. 'The alleged abuse began while Kos was a student at Holy

Trinity seminary in Dallas, and continued during placements at three different churches. The Dallas diocese was found guilty of failing to take seriously scores of abuse allegations . . . Shortly after the first complaints he was promoted to pastor.'[4] In awarding vast sums in damages to the victims of the abuse, the jury agreed that the Dallas diocese had not taken the reported allegations seriously and had ignored evidence. Despite claims by the diocese that they were not responsible for the actions of their priest, this defence was not accepted.

In Scotland, there have been 300 separate claims for damages for abuse from former child residents of Nazareth House children's homes in Aberdeen and Cardonald. These homes were run by Roman Catholic nuns, the Sisters of Nazareth, and the abuse is alleged to have taken place throughout the 1960s and 1970s. Most of the victims were girls. The range of horrific abuse on these young children – aged from three to fifteen years of age – included some children stating they had been sexually abused from the age of eight years.

In the *Aberdeen Press and Journal*, Bishop Mario Conti 'expressed concern that the reputation of the church had been tarnished', and in a quest for justice was canvassing former residents who had good memories of their time at Nazareth House to write in to him, not just those who had complaints.[5] It is unclear how justice for the children who were abused could be aided by former residents, who were presumably not abused, writing to the bishop. The implication is that the bishop is much more concerned about justice for the Sisters of Nazareth, their reputation and perhaps even more importantly the reputation of the Roman Catholic Church, than the destruction of the lives of so many children. Indeed, subsequent press reports have confirmed the bishop's decision to stand by the order, and have also quoted the Poor Sisters of Nazareth as claiming that the 300 former residents who have sought compensation for their abusive experiences are attempting to elicit money through moral blackmail.[6] I would question the bishop's priorities, and suggest that the Church would improve its reputation more by accepting responsibility for and complicity in the crimes against these children.

These examples highlight some of the reactions of churches when abuse is alleged against members of the clergy or congregation. There is a sense of shock and disbelief. There is good reason to believe that most child sexual abuse perpetrated by priests and ministers of religion is kept hidden, both in terms of children not disclosing and congregational members not suspecting – being unable to suspend disbelief – that such a thing could happen. No minister of God would do such a thing.

There may also be feelings of betrayal – by the Church, by God – and disillusionment. Shock and disbelief may turn to anger and rage towards the perpetrator, and a desire for punishment and justice. They may have feelings of inadequacy and exploitation. How could I have trusted, how could I not have suspected, how could I have befriended the abuser? Also, adults who may have suspected that sexual abuse might be being perpetrated may well have reason to cover it up, at least in terms of not allowing it to reach the ears of those outside the Church, so that their possible complicity is not exposed. In this way neither they nor the Church will be tainted. Or they may have feelings of guilt and shame that they were insufficiently supportive in the past, and thereby to some degree culpable, and want now to support the perpetrator, which leads them (perhaps through good intentions) to try to find superficial solutions.

One myth that seems to have been widely believed in some church circles is that the sexual abuse of children is just an inappropriate response to stress, which can be resolved by sending the offender away for a period of quiet prayer and contemplation. This assumes that the offending behaviour was just a temporary aberration.[7]

There is biblical justification for this response within Matthew: 'If your brother sins against you, go and show him his fault, just between the two of you. If he listens to you, you have won your brother over. But if he will not listen, take one or two others along, so that every matter may be established by the testimony of two or three witnesses. If he refuses to listen to them, tell it to the church; and if he refuses to listen even to the church, treat him as you would a pagan or a tax collector' (Matthew 18:15–17).

It is not surprising that child sexual abuse allegations have come to light no more readily when perpetrated by priests and ministers of religion than when perpetrated by parents. Power and responsibility are located within the role of priest. This power is backed by adults who form the management and congregations of the churches. The Church is God's representative on earth, and the minister its mediator to the congregation. How could a child defy what was perpetrated in the Lord's name? Yet again, how can a child tell?

This is echoed when the abuse is committed by a female member of the ministry, such as a nun, or another prominent member of the church congregation. While the male priest can be seen by the child in God the Father's image, the female may be seen in the image of the Madonna. The child, who has experienced sexual abuse perpetrated by a woman whose religious image is of someone who is neither sexual nor powerful (meek, mild and virginal

Mary), and who enshrines pure maternalism (Mary, mother of God), is presented with great confusion and great guilt. The child who is abused within a religious context has tempted, tainted and sinned against God. The child is evil, demonic. Again, how can a child tell? And who in the Church would suspend their (dis)belief to believe the child?

Indeed, there are few cases of child sexual abuse perpetrated within the Church that are brought to court, let alone subjected to the scrutiny of two or three witnesses – and as indicated above the cases that are brought by victims of sexual abuse are more generally civil actions for damages rather than criminal prosecutions. Meanwhile there are a significant number of other child sexual abuse allegations that result in 'damages' being paid out of court, particularly in the United States of America, and the matter is left at that. It seems more like buying silence, although it is an admission of responsibility and culpability, an acknowledgement of what actually happened, which can be an essential base for the healing of the sexually abused child, even if the offence was some years before and the child is by now an adult. I will consider the aspects of restitution, compensation and retribution later.

Moreover, if the abuser does acknowledge his sins, and wants a fresh start, perhaps after a period of reflection on retreat to help re-establish his approach to ministry and resolve his problems as a priest (rather than as a sexual criminal), there is often a resort to the so-called 'geographical solution', where (as mentioned above) the abuser is moved to another part of the country or even another country.

The Primus of the Scottish Episcopal Church, in a book that I will refer to positively later, exposes the weakness of even the informed liberal theological argument.

The abuse and exploitation of children is the most distressing aspect of human sexual history, and it is one of the most difficult to deal with. There is some evidence that compulsive paedophilia can be altered by intensive therapy, though very few penal institutions anywhere offer this service. To use a genetic analogy, the only really hopeful approach is to purge this distressing mutation from the human system by taking all possible steps to remove children from situations of abuse so that they will not, as adults, replicate the behaviour that scarred them as children.[8]

While Holloway acknowledges the possible cycle of abuse, the lack of treatment facilities for imprisoned paedophiles (only the tip of an enormous iceberg) is the excuse for his proposal of another kind of 'geographical solution' – this time removing the children from the homes and presence of their abusers rather than the perpetrators of abuse from their victims. This echoes the pre-Children Act position, which has rightly been seen as punitive of the victims. It also fails to acknowledge the scale of abuse. To where are we to consign the one in four girls and one in seven boys who have been abused?

The consequences for some perpetrators of child sexual abuse who, whether in the absence of other services, or in anticipation of a more favourable and forgiving response than that provided by secular authorities, have turned to the Church for healing is that they have been subjected to deliverance ministry whereby the demon is cast out of the offender. Rather than face and own up to their responsibilities as offenders, it is the devil within them that is blamed and removed. Their actions were the workings of their possession by evil. Therefore, as offenders, and subsequently as saved souls, they are detached from any part of their responsibility as human beings for their previous actions.

A different, but no less worrying, response by churches to abusers who turn to them for help is the naive and swift acceptance of the perpetrator as a reformed sinner, who by confessing – however partial and minimalist the confession – is somehow restored to a life of faith and goodness. These offenders – and it is well to remember that that is what they are, for they have not just committed a sin but have actually committed crimes – are often transformed readily into ardent exponents of the Christian message, and willingly undertake outreach to some of the more vulnerable members of the church congregation. Some churches have allowed, or even encouraged, the perpetrator to become actively involved with children in the church setting. Without considering here the risks that such actions may expose other children to, it is enough to reflect on how the previous victims of that abuser may view the church that welcomes so willingly the person who perpetrated the abuse.

I am unclear whether this meets the injunction to treat the abuser as a 'pagan or a tax collector', although it is well to remember that Matthew was himself a tax collector who left his job and followed Jesus. Through following Jesus he left the work of the devil. He was delivered; he was reformed. This quote, then, may have particular resonance for Matthew, and especially so when Matthew refers later to another teaching of Jesus: 'Jesus said to them, "I tell you the truth, the tax collectors and the prostitutes are entering the kingdom of God ahead of you. For John came to you to show you the way of righteousness, and you did not believe him, but the tax collectors and the prostitutes did"' (Matthew 21:31–32).

This reference to one of Jesus' sayings can also be difficult for a survivor of abuse, as are other references to sinners entering heaven, and the mission of Christ and

Christians being to save sinners. To what extent, then, have victims of child sexual abuse had their bodies used as a vehicle for the subsequent repentance and salvation of their abusers, the sinners?

I will now turn to the second issue, that of forgiveness. Church leaders may have a confusion of desires to excuse and to forgive the perpetrator, and in so doing may put the victim under pressure to forgive the abuser. Forgiveness is a central concern of any Christian who is wanting to help themselves or someone else recover from childhood sexual abuse. It is also a terrible burden on the survivor, and can inhibit healing. I will quote again from Matthew: 'Then Peter came to Jesus and asked, "Lord, how many times shall I forgive my brother when he sins against me? Up to seven times?" Jesus answered, "I tell you, not seven times, but seventy-seven times"' (Matthew 18:21–22).

Can a child be expected to forgive his or her abusers, for abuse that may be perpetrated on seventy-seven occasions? Indeed, even being angry about the abuse seems to be proscribed: 'You have heard that it was said to the people long ago, "Do not murder, and anyone who murders will be subject to judgment." But I tell you that anyone who is angry with his brother will be subject to judgment' (Matthew 5:21–22).

Moreover, the price of not forgiving is condemnation by God. In the parable which Jesus used to illustrate to Peter the need for forgiveness, the master who had remitted his servant's enormous debt was outraged to learn that the same servant had shown no pity on one of his own debtors. 'In anger his master turned him over to the jailers to be tortured, until he should pay back all he owed. That is how my heavenly Father will treat each of you unless you forgive your brother from your heart' (Matthew 18:34–35).

The pressure on survivors of child sexual abuse to forgive their abusers is enormous. This is partly external pressure: family, friends, clergy and fellow Christians may all exalt the benefits of forgiveness. Is this pressure based on unconditional love for the survivor? Or is it to help these other secondary victims heal? For if children who have been abused can move forward and recover from their abuse, as demonstrated by the releasing of their pain through forgiveness, then we can all move on. This may also suggest that the secondary victims are also the secondary perpetrators. They share complicity in the abuse, and seek the signs of forgiveness to release them from their burden of guilt and responsibility. I know too how I have desperately wanted my children to heal. I have felt trapped, unable to move forward in my life unless and until they recover. Am I seeking their forgiveness? Am I part of this pressure on them to forgive?

The other pressure is internalised. In the desperation to recover from the abuse, the failure to feel a true sense of forgiveness compounds the issues. The survivors may feel further guilt and responsibility for their failure to recover, as demonstrated by their inability to come to terms with the need to forgive. They may have found it hard enough to express their anger at their abusers, and they now feel further guilt that they have this anger, that it is unhealthy, even that it needs to be transformed into compassion.

The pressure on a survivor to forgive is a further form of abuse.

Many women try desperately to forgive. Survivors have often said how stuck they feel. They despair for their complete healing, because they can't foresee forgiving the person who abused them. But, as Ellen says in her workshops, 'Why should you? First they steal everything else from you and

then they want forgiveness too? Let them get their own.
You've given enough'.[9]

While it may always be hard to forgive, there is no doubt it
is more excruciatingly difficult to forgive when the abusers
show no acknowledgement of or regret for their actions,
or when they are continuing to abuse. How can victims of
abuse forgive at the very moment the abuse is happening?
Can we hope to be like Jesus, who was able to forgive his
executioners during his crucifixion, according to later ver-
sions of Luke's Gospel?

However, Jesus qualified his forgiveness on the cross:
'Father, forgive them, for they do not know what they are
doing' (Luke 23:24). Can children accept that the adults,
who may be their parents, who are perpetrating sexual
abuse on them do not know what they are doing?

This leads me to the third area I wish to explore. Perhaps it is ordained that children should suffer at the hands
of their parents and families; and that suffering is necessary for those who would be Christians. 'Do not suppose
that I have come to bring peace to the earth. I did not
come to bring peace, but a sword. For I have come to turn
"a man against his father, a daughter against her mother,
a daughter-in-law against her mother-in-law – a man's
enemies will be the members of his own household"'
(Matthew 10:34–36).

Meanwhile, in the sermon on the mount, the rewards of
persecution for those who follow Jesus are outlined:
'Blessed are those who are persecuted because of righteousness, for theirs is the kingdom of heaven. Blessed are
you when people insult you, persecute you and falsely say
all kinds of evil against you because of me. Rejoice and be
glad, because great is your reward in heaven, for in the

same way they persecuted the prophets who were before you' (Matthew 5:10–12).

The victim who takes this literally may begin to thrive in their abuse, seeing it as a necessary sacrifice of their body in their search for a deeper spirituality, a closeness to God. They have discovered a Christian mission in being a victim, even a victim to death. 'Do not be afraid of those who kill the body but cannot kill the soul. Rather, be afraid of the One who can destroy both soul and body in hell' (Matthew 10:28). The self-loathing of victims of sexual abuse is deep enough, and many have strong feelings that they would be better off dead, without having a spiritual confirmation or justification of this. Clearly we need to reconsider this interpretation of the Gospels.

This exploration of the filth and the faith has raised major issues with the way the Chuch has dealt with the whole arena of child sexual abuse, and how the interpretation of the Gospels has compounded and confused the difficulties for survivors. As in previous chapters, I am left with less than satisfactory answers. In both secular and spiritual terms, we are failing children, and hence each other, dreadfully. We are not grasping the fundamental issues that permeate our human relationships, and our spiritual connectedness. I will return to reconsider the scope for Christians, within and outside the Church, to respond to the needs of perpetrators and survivors of abuse in the following chapters. At this point I want readers to identify with me as I ask these basic questions.

How can we reach out spiritually to those so sorely betrayed, whose souls have been desecrated, without appearing to deny or minimise their experiences; and without legitimising their pain as a human sacrifice, the necessary suffering of God's disciples?

Is it realistic, and is it fair, to sexually abused children, and to adults who have been abused as children, and to the 'secondary victims' (the carers, friends and relatives of abusers and those they have abused), to ask them to have faith in God? In particular to have faith in a God who seems to be contradictory, on the one hand threatening punishment to those who abuse children, but on the other putting extra burdens on those who have been abused by demanding the forgiveness of their abusers, and prioritising the salvation of sinners?

'Do not mock us; grief has made us unbelieving –
  We look up for God, but tears have made us blind.'
Do you hear the children weeping and disproving,
  O my brothers, what ye preach?
For God's possible is taught by His world's loving,
  And the children doubt of each.[10]

CHAPTER 8

REVELATIONS

My questions

What do sexually abused children need from adults?
How do we help children break out of the cycle of abuse?
How can we support children who have been abused?
Can sexually abused children find a relationship with God?

In this chapter I will give some answers based on what my academic research, and my personal and professional experiences, have revealed to me.

Revelations can arise from a momentary flash of inspiration, or from painstaking research across many fields; from a chance meeting or a remark which highlights a different context or perspective; or from reflection on previous experiences not fully understood at the time. Revelations may be less original ideas, more old ideas put together in new ways. They are always powerful, as they interrupt patterns of beliefs and thoughts often long established. Revelations also impact powerfully on the emotions: they can be ecstatically joyful and horrifically dreadful, both at the same time. Indeed, the spiritual dimension of revelations brings us closer to our understanding of God, with all the attendant fear and joy of such an encounter. Revelations are not welcomed by the faint of heart, nor by the comfortable and complacent, nor always by the desperate; for they invoke new actions, new energy, new risks. Revelations are about fundamental change.

I will attempt to separate out some of these revelations into particular themes, although the reader will be aware that all these themes must interrelate.

1. Support strategies for children

I will consider what children need. I will also be clear about what children don't need. How we conduct and support ourselves as adults, to meet both our needs and our children's needs, will be expored more in the next chapter. But, as Alice Miller writes, first and foremost we need to believe that a non-abusing world is possible for our children. 'It is perfectly possible to awaken from sleep and, in that waking state, to be open to messages from our children that can help us never again to destroy life but rather to protect it and allow it to blossom.'[1]

Sexually abused children are quite clear about what they want. They don't seek retribution, they don't need the abuser to be punished, they don't yearn for compensation. What they want is *justice*. How can we understand, then, what they mean by justice and how that justice is to be achieved?

Punishment for wrong-doing is the societal norm when we talk of justice. But we have already seen that convictions for sexual abuse are rare. Punishment is an unlikely outcome for abusers. What we also need to keep in mind is the impact on children when their abusers are punished. Understandably, these children believe that they have brought about this verdict, and that they are now responsible for the suffering of another human being, often an adult whom they needed and wanted to love and care for them. It is not uncommon for abusers, accused by their victims, to fall ill, sometimes seriously so. The family may split up as a consequence of the allegations of abuse, and children can experience themselves effectively as abusers of their abusers, as well as being victims again, in that they may be deprived of a chance to restore, reclaim or establish non-abusive relationships.

Therefore, the consequences of an abuser being punished as a direct result of the child's testimony may be dreadful for the child, emotionally, socially and spiritually. The outcome may be far from what the child wants and needs. Those who support a child in the aftermath of a conviction need to pay attention not only to the child's recovery from the abuse but their recovery from the punishment inflicted on the abuser.

Retribution, and its close associate retaliation, are linked to punishment. The notion of 'an eye for an eye' can be terrifying for children. They do not want or need the power to inflict harm on adults. It is a burden, not a release. It is not appropriate empowerment. The anger that leads to retaliation and retribution, and ultimately to sexual abuse and murder, is exactly what Jesus spoke against in Matthew 5: 21–26. It is destructive, not constructive anger. Moreover, it can become cyclical. If the retribution is too great, the child's fear of the abuser coming back to 'get them' is overwhelming. This is exactly the dread in which many children live once they have disclosed the abuse, the fear of retribution. It is in no way a positive experience, and is generally at least as damaging as the abuse. Indeed, it is a perpetuation of the abuse. Punishment and retribution, then, are not what children mean by justice.

Litigation through civil court cases has become a significant means of obtaining a sense of justice. While there is a real issue of 'blood money', in terms of how much an act of sexual abuse is worth, or what price can be placed on the loss and destruction of childhood, the main argument in its favour is the formal recognition of what actually happened to the child, the legitimation of the reality of their experiences, in a context where very few children can experience that confirmation within the criminal justice system. Litigation has become enshrined in the Children (Scotland) Act 1995, whereby a child can sue parents for their failure to fulfil their parental responsibilities to have their health, development and welfare as paramount considerations. Failure to protect children from abuse, neglect or exploitation is one obvious ground for litigation.

The Criminal Injuries Compensation Board in Britain fulfils a similar function in respect of that legitimation role. For compensation to be awarded the Criminal Injuries Compensation Board does not require a perpetrator to be convicted, or even charged and prosecuted, in recognition of the fact that convictions are not viable in most cases of child sexual abuse. That is, this scheme formally acknowledges the failings of the criminal justice system, and for the children who receive awards this effectively compensates as much for the failure of that system as for the abuse perpetrated.

For my children, who were awarded money by the Criminal Injuries Compensation Board, it was almost insignificant that different amounts were given to the two of them, and that a monetary value could actually be placed on their experiences. For them the importance lay in the fact that they had been believed, while in the criminal justice system they had been effectively disbelieved. No charges had been levelled, no prosecution undertaken, no conviction determined, no admission of culpability made. Given the presumption of innocence of those accused until proven guilty, children are presumed guilty of telling lies, falsely accusing their perpetrators. But the Criminal Injuries Compensation Board believed them.

One of my children could make no claim from the Criminal Injuries Compensation Board as she had not been sexually abused. While this was an accurate reflection of her history, in that no crime had been perpetrated against her, she too had been severely affected by what had happened to her sister and brother, and the implications for all their childhoods. This emphasises again how the impact of child sexual abuse is not confined to those who have been victims. Others who are witness to (or who are intimately involved with) the victims, and who are critical to their survival, as my daughter was to her sister and brother, can be deeply traumatised by their experiences too. Likewise, for the non-abused child who has a parent who is an alleged abuser, this too can have traumatic effects.

Justice, then, is much more than compensation. Children do want justice, but of a different kind from that normally understood in the adult world. Children need something greater, which legitimises their experiences, even as secondary victims, and which helps their survival. For the opportunity to grow, to thrive intellectually, physically, emotionally, socially and spiritually, must be the ultimate goal of justice for *all* children.

The justice children crave is threefold:

- they want an acknowledgement of what they have experienced, and that it has been abusive;
- they want the perpetrator to acknowledge the impact of what has been done, and – ideally – to show some care, concern and empathy for them;
- they want the abuse to stop.

The current response from adults is to offer them everything else instead (in terms of punishment, retribution and compensation) or, generally, nothing at all. This compounds a child's sense and experience of injustice. One of the most damaging aspects of a child's experience of the abuse is for the perpetrator to deny it has happened; and to vilify the child who has spoken out; and for the abuse to continue, or (if not actually continuing) for it potentially to happen again. Children are astute: even a young child can realise that if abuse has taken place, and hasn't been admitted, it is likely to recur.

I recall clearly and painfully how my son experienced the betrayal by one of his abusers when she denied what she had done. All he wanted was for her to acknowledge that what she had been doing hurt and scared him, that she was sorry for hurting him, and that she would not do it again. However simplistic that may seem, it was absolutely vital. It was everything that he needed and he wanted. He got none of these things. Instead he got entrapped in both the criminal justice and civil court systems, as they lumbered abusively onwards. Never did these legal systems show any understanding of or interest in what he needed and deserved, which were these three essential and elemental preconditions for human renewal – the acknowledgement by the abuser of his suffering, an apology for the hurt inflicted, and a promise that it would not recur. Instead he got denial and dismissal, first from the abusers, and then from the participants in the legal systems.

His trauma, which was already devastating his entire being, deepened. His despair overtook his body and mind. That he survived was – and continues to be – miraculous.

2. Breaking the cycle of abuse

Crucial in our resolve to promote the welfare of children, then, must be our determination to overturn notions of justice which perpetuate and exacerbate the problem, and which fail to fulfil the criteria set out by children in terms of what they need. Central to this strategy is the need to break the cycle of abuse, as I outlined it earlier. I reproduce the diagram here.

The adult notions of justice, whether based on Roman or Judaic law, involve the punisher, who is effectively the legitimate (as opposed to the illegitimate) persecutor. They

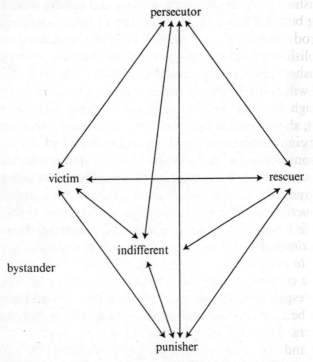

Figure 6.   The expanded cycle of abuse in operation

require a victim for a conviction to be obtained; and the greater the victimisation the greater the punishment that can be meted out. The less empowered the victim, the more the legitimation for the rescuer, who perpetuates the disempowerment of the victim. If there is a paucity of evidence to charge, prosecute and convict a perpetrator, this leads to indifference shown to the child who has been abused. There is no justice recognisable by children in this cycle. It is, rightly, a cycle of abuse, and to the extent that we collude with it we share complicitly in the sexual abuse of children.

The politics of abolition[2] state that if a system, policy, law or institution is harmful or destructive it should be abolished. There is no need to wait until there is something better with which to replace it. Indeed, this is counterproductive. There will be little possibility of establishing anything better until the present system is abolished, as those with vested interests in the status quo will attempt to ensure its continuance. It is only through abolition that we become free to see what, if anything, should be put in place to meet the needs manifestly not being met by the system that was abolished.

I consider myself to be on very safe ground when I state, unequivocally, that *an horrifically expensive criminal justice system which children and non-abusing parents find destructive and abusive, which is based on roles which are the life-blood of the cycle of abuse, and which only convicts an estimated one per cent of child sexual abusers, has no right to exist.*

The criminal justice system is not to be tinkered with in the desperate hope of some marginal improvement. It must be abolished from all contact with child sexual abuse matters. This one act alone would prevent harm to children and their non-abusing parents and carers who suffer system abuse. What could be achieved with the money saved is beyond even my dreams. It certainly could be used to promote a supportive framework for social justice.

Justice for children requires them not to be victims. This is more than just not being abused again. It means they can walk down the street without feeling that they have a label on their heads saying 'victim of sexual abuse'. It means that their experiences can be acknowledged without the stigma. The experience is a terrible enough fact, without it being a source of further trauma due to the incomprehension, suspicion, disgust, shame, guilt, fear and pity engendered in the adult environment for the abused child. In effect, what we need to do to support children is to 'normalise' them and their abuse, to see their experiences as being dreadful, destructive, unacceptable, but not taboo. There is a need to hear the children cry, and to accept them and their abuse. This act of reaching out and acceptance is an essential element of the healing balm.

Justice for children means not being ignored, dismissed or treated with indifference as if their experiences were of a lesser order, or that they will forget all about their abuse when they are older. It means adults putting a value on children that is not about property and possession, but about our social and spiritual essence. There is no greater benchmark for our civilisation than the way we treat our children.

Justice for children also means not having to be rescued. The burden for meeting children's needs must lie in the adult world, but the way in which this is undertaken does not presume children should be disabled from expressing their views, and stating their wishes with respect to their bodies, their living situation, their relationships.

To break the cycle of abuse we need to equalise our relationships. We are all children of God; we are all brothers and sisters in and of Christ. This means we do not set ourselves above each other. The cycle of abuse is based on unequal relationships. The perpetrator is 'one-up' on the victim, as is the rescuer and indifferent. The punisher is 'one-up' on the persecutor. These roles are disabling, as is the role of bystander in its various forms. Each of these roles, as adopted by us when we get hooked into the cycle of abuse, allows us to avoid taking responsibility for our own actions. In any of these roles we can deny what we are doing. No, we are not persecutors. No, we are not victims. No, we are not indifferent. No, we are not punishers; and so on.

Or we explain away and excuse our actions. We persecute because the victim deserves it, because someone else hasn't met our needs, because we're ill, or because we too have previously been victimised; what we hide is that we are expressing our self-loathing. We rescue because the victim needs us to save them, because they are too weak, useless, powerless to manage without us; what we hide is that we need them to be emotionally dependent on us. We punish because the persecutor needs to be given a lesson, to deter other potential persecutors, to make sure they don't get away with it; what we hide is our fear that we too could be culpable. We are indifferent because we are of a different social class, status or situation, because we are adults, because we have more important things to do; what we hide is our fear of taking responsibility for facing up to pain.

We can break the cycle of abuse by refusing to play these games, and therefore not presenting these roles as models for our children. The difficulty for us is, of course, that these roles are well embedded in our psyche through our social upbringing, and reinforced in our everyday psychological responses to relationship interactions, and through the media representations of 'normal' role responses. There is clear evidence, unfortunately, in the

nature and extent of abusive relationships that character-
ise much of our social interaction. The sexual abuse of
children, however appalling and extensive, is but one manifestation of this.

This emphasises the need to break the bystanding patterns within our society. The first step to achieve this is to
rediscover empathy and inter-connectedness. We live in a
society which, due to the extent of our own personal suffering, and the influence of media presentations of suffering, has left many of us desensitised to the pain of others.
We are increasingly detached. We need to walk in each
other's shoes, to rediscover our relationships with each
other. Part of this is to address our beliefs. Western society
has heralded notions of individualism, of everyone's independence; yet if we assess how independent we actually are
we realise that there is so little that we can do to ensure our
own survival without the work and support of others. We
all need people to service us. To that extent we have become
incredibly dependent. But we also contribute by working
to support others. Therefore, albeit in a somewhat
detached, administrative and indirect way, we are interdependent. Interdependence is a powerful form of relationship. Recognising our interdependence allows us to reclaim
a moral purpose for us all, not as isolated individuals but
as fellow human beings. We are brothers and sisters.

The second step is to recognise that we are already
involved in injustice and suffering through our interdependence. We share complicity. Doing nothing contributes to
the existence and perpetuation of injustice and suffering.
To this extent it is a fact, however frightening, that we
cannot be innocent bystanders. Our complicity, by which
I do not infer culpability, implies our responsibility for
intervention towards resolution. 'Understanding and
accepting personal responsibility for bystanding behaviour

may be deeply uncomfortable knowledge. The questions raised by these issues tap into some very deep, primitive roots having to do with survival.'[3] I will later consider ways in which we can move beyond survival.

The third step is to recognise that actions are not value-free. All actions (and non-actions) have a basis in explicit or implicit values and beliefs. Therefore, the combination of these three steps helps us understand that we have an inter-connectedness with and a responsibility to all our fellow human beings; that we are already involved with them; and the way we are involved has a moral basis. If we consider the moral basis of our involvement, we can ask ourselves: does it reflect the way we would want to be? As Christians, are our actions and relationships based on the beliefs and values we hold dear?

It is not a case of morally justifying our involvement in intervening to support children who are suffering, and protecting children from abuse; that justification precedes us. It is a case of morally opposing our actions based on notions of independence, separateness, detachment and irresponsibility which allow us to be bystanders and thereby to collude with the abuse being inflicted. We are responsible for our child care and for our criminal justice system. We need to adopt compassionate and empathic actions in relationship to all children: actions based on values which acknowledge our collective and individual responsibility. It is about standing by each other, rather than bystanding.

There is one well-known text that conveys completely the essence of Christian care and support. It shows how bystanding is based on un-Christian values. It breaks with conventional religious, legal and ethical codes. It recognises our inter-connectedness, beyond biology and culture. It demonstrates empathy and compassion.

A man was going down from Jerusalem to Jericho, when he fell into the hands of robbers. They stripped him of his clothes, beat him and went away, leaving him halfdead. A priest happened to be going down the same road, and when he saw the man, he passed by on the other side. So too, a Levite, when he came to the place and saw him, passed by on the other side. But a Samaritan, as he travelled, came where the man was; and when he saw him he took pity on him. He went to him, bandaged his wounds, pouring on oil and wine. Then he put the man on his donkey, brought him to an inn and took care of him. The next day he took out two silver coins and gave them to the innkeeper. 'Look after him,' he said, 'and when I return, I will reimburse you for any extra expense you may have.'

'Which of these three do you think was a neighbour to the man who fell into the hands of robbers?'

The expert in the law replied, 'The one who had mercy on him.'

Jesus told him, 'Go and do likewise.'

Luke 10:30–37

3. Christian child care

The parable of the good Samaritan is a model for our Christian child care as well as our relationships with other adults. But what does that mean for our relationships with children? My starting point is that children are not, and must not be, expected to take responsibility for their own child care. This is not to say they should be treated with anything other than the utmost respect and love that any human being deserves – quite the opposite. But it is to remove the burden of responsibility for meeting their needs, which is the province of the adult world, from them.

At present, civil and private law in Western countries either emphasises parental rights or attempts a balance between rights and responsibilities. However, this balance is always uneven, given the power imbalance between adults and children. It is the parental responsibilities that must be the determining factor, and the rights must not conflict with these responsibilities. We need also to ask, whose children are they? To whom do we give parental responsibilities?

The answer can be found in recognising our relationship to God, which holds us as interdependent and individually and collectively responsible for our children. This is an awesome concept, and its practical application will find opponents. The arguments will include: I brought this child into the world and I have the right to bring it up in the way I want; I don't want other adults involved – after all, they might abuse my child; I have a special bond with my child as I created it; I want my child to have a special relationship with me, as that's what all children need.

These arguments don't hold much water. First, the argument in favour of possession and control due to birth immediately sounds abusive. Irrespective of who gave birth to the child, that child has as much right to love and care, and freedom from abuse, as any child.

Secondly, the fear of other adults' involvement, as they may abuse the child, denies again that it is generally those who bring up the children, and who often have biological connections with the child, who are the most frequent abusers.

Thirdly, other adults are involved. One of the guide-lines to help survivors of abuse, which I believe is as applicable to all children, is – *encourage the child to use other support as well as you*. For example, most parents rely on teachers to educate their children; and friends, neighbours and relatives to child-mind. It is possible and desirable that these extra-familial supports are well established and nurturing.

Fourthly, it is important that a child does feel a special

bond with an adult, which is mutually experienced. Bearing a child is not the only way to achieve that. The most obvious example is adoption; I can testify to the bond that can be achieved between an adopted boy and his new parents. Another case would be when love and care given by the new partner of either parent. In my own experience, my children's stepmother has shown, notwithstanding all the enormous efforts and difficulties she inherited from their past, that she can attain the highest form of bonding for children whose early childhood she missed. Some experiences of collective child care produce similar accounts of strong bonds.

Christian child care has to be based on love, and that is the only criterion that counts. I use Peck's definition of love as a basis: 'The will to extend one's self for the purpose of nurturing one's own or another's spiritual growth'.[4] The role of parenting, which can be shared between a number of adults, and be extended to a number of children, has to be based on the *act* of love. It is neither just, nor primarily, a feeling. It is a spiritual commitment. It is important that parenting responsibilities are shared. First, it is unreasonable to expect one or two adults to be able to promote adequately the growth in a child – including spiritual growth – alone. Secondly, it is important that the child experiences the love of a number of adults, which allows the child to turn to one of them in times of stress or confusion. In effect, it provides opportunities for a child to realise that abuse is not love and that there is someone to whom the child can turn to find support.

4. The search for truth, not proof

Children need to be taken seriously, and for me – even if not for Lord Clyde whose comments I quoted in chapter 1 – that *does* mean being believed.

Children do not get hung up on proof, but they are strong on truth. Children can become very hurt, disillusioned and damaged at the suggestion that they are not telling the truth. They do not have the same need of evidence; they know what's true. The adult world, particularly in the West, demands certainty and eschews doubt which is its opposite. Certainty requires proof; proof requires evidence. The rational/scientific paradigm struggles to accept that truth can lie outside of proof and certainty.

Yet this is what children know. It is also the basis of our spirituality. As Christians we have faith. Faith encapsulates doubt; it is therefore the opposite of certainty. We cannot prove that God exists, although often we feel obliged to scrabble around for evidence to meet demands (from ourselves or from other doubters or mockers). We know it as a truth, because we have faith. That also means we have doubts too. In the New Testament Philip had doubts, and could not understand the concept of Jesus as truth.

Jesus answered, 'I am the way and the truth and the life. No-one comes to the Father except through me. If you really knew me, you would know my Father as well. From now on, you do know him and have seen him.'

Philip said, 'Lord, show us the Father and that will be enough for us.'

Jesus answered: 'Don't you know me, Philip, even after I have been among you such a long time? Anyone who has seen me has seen the Father. How can you say, "Show us the Father"? Don't you believe that I am in the Father and the Father is in me? The words I say to you are not just my own. Rather, it is the Father, living in me, who is doing his work. Believe me when I say that I am in the Father and the Father is in me; or at least believe on the evidence of the

miracles themselves. I tell you the truth, anyone who has
faith in me will do what I have been doing.'

John 14:6–12

The evidence of the miracles, themselves open to disbelief from those seeking rational/scientific confirmation,
are of secondary importance. Belief in the truth was of the
greatest importance. Being a witness to truth was essential
for Jesus, whereas for Pilate truth, unlike evidence, could
not be weighed:

'You are a king, then!' said Pilate
    Jesus answered, 'You are right in saying I am a king. In
fact, for this reason I was born, and for this I came into the
world, to testify to the truth. Everyone on the side of truth
listens to me.'
    'What is truth?' Pilate asked. With this he went out again to
the Jews and said, 'I find no basis for a charge against him.'

John 18:37–38

In an age which, at least in academic circles, is questioning the rational/scientific paradigm, and which is
describing our era as post-modernist, there is a welcome
resurgence of credibility given to truth, beliefs and values,
rather than empiricism and evidential proof.

5. The problem of self-loathing – victims and perpetrators

I consider self-loathing to be the single most destructive
and significant outcome of child sexual abuse for the victim. This is also true for those I refer to as the secondary
victims (the non-abusing parents, carers, siblings and
friends of victims, and the families and friends of perpetrators). It is crucial that we recognise how greatly these
secondary victims are affected, in order that we may

appreciate their need for and use of survival strategies. There is also a wider societal impact, which could be conceived as producing tertiary victims (a concept I am introducing here to refer to the impact on communities that are affected by widespread sexual abuse, even though they do not know personally the victims or perpetrators). If my contention is right that self-loathing is the single most significant outcome of child sexual abuse on victims – that is, primary, secondary and tertiary victims – then we can begin to see the enormity of the problem we have to address. The ripples in the social pond spread wide every time a child is sexually abused.

Alice Miller writes powerfully about the impact that parents have on their children, and we can see how what she says applies when that parenting inculcates a deeply held sense of self-loathing. The motivation for the parental behaviour is self-loathing, and it has a similar effect on the child's self-belief. This can be passed on from generation to generation until and unless there is a conscious willingness to acknowledge and address the cycle.

> The suffering that was not consciously felt as a child can be avoided by delegating it to one's own children . . . (Parents) encounter their own humiliating past in the child's eyes, and they ward it off with the power they now have. We cannot, simply by an act of will, free ourselves from repeating the patterns of our parents' behaviour – which we had to learn very early in life. We become free of them only when we can fully feel and acknowledge the suffering they inflicted on us. We can only then become fully aware of these patterns and condemn them, unequivocally.[5]

Self-loathing is a prominent feature of adults with mental

health difficulties, and not surprisingly the connection between childhood sexual abuse and adult mental health problems (including self-mutilation and substance abuse) is being increasingly recognised.

6. From self-loathing to developing a child's self-love

Our support strategies for children who have been sexually abused must fundamentally appreciate the impact the abuse has had on them in terms of self-esteem and self-loathing – on their ability to love themselves. Anyone who has experienced the difficulty of loving and caring for a child who doubts within their soul that they are lovable will recognise the enormity of the task required of us. The consistency of acceptance of them as persons created in God's image and nurturing their spiritual growth is a trial for us. The efforts expended by sexually abused children to hook us into one of the roles in the cycle of abuse is powerful. They will find our 'buttons' and press them. We will want to punish them; to rescue them; to be indifferent to them; to persecute them. Sometimes we find ourselves victims to them.

I will look more closely at how we can find support to help us address our own self-loathing and resist our own potential to become abusive as adults, parents and as communities of Christians, in the next chapter. At present the focus is on support strategies for children, and in trying to identify what sexually abused children need we must not lose sight of the fact that we do not, and undoubtedly will not, always know which child has or has not been abused. The statistics of abuse may have frightened us. We may mentally check off the numbers of children we know, and estimate on the basis of the percentages of those likely to be abused just how many of them may actually be suffering

sexual abuse – unknown to us, and under our noses, perpetrated by adults who may well be our relations or those we
consider good friends. Again I will consider this factor
further in the next chapter.

Given our ignorance of the extent of sexual abuse due
to the survival strategies of children which hide the disclosure of abuse within a societal context based on an
abusive criminal justice system, the important point here
is that the support strategies I propose need to be applied
to *all* children.

If we reconsider the guide-lines of good practice in
helping adult survivors recover from their childhood sexual abuse, as detailed in Chapter 6, there are three that are
immediately applicable not only to the needs of sexually
abused children but to all children. These are:

Believe survivors – children rarely make up stories of abuse

This is the first need of children who have been sexually
abused, and is crucial to their potential to recover, even
though it does not fit into the legalised, criminal investiga-
tions-based approach. As I argued earlier, denial and disbelief of a child's experiences by adults are very damaging
and abusive. But no child should have to be disbelieved.
Telling lies is a survival strategy of those who have experienced fear at telling the truth. The onset of a child telling
lies (or at least hiding the truth) may well reflect the onset
of self-loathing.

Acknowledge that the child has been damaged by the abuse

This is the second of the three needs of children who have
been sexually abused, and this acknowledgement is best
combined with:

Express your compassion

It would be ideal if the abuser could, directly or indirectly, express compassion for the child too. All children deserve to have their experiences validated, whether or not they may be deemed to be abusive, and that means not just acknowledging what happened but how they felt about it. Children have a strong sense of justice, in terms of what's fair and what's right. It may not coincide with the kind of materialistic parity we normally adopt when we think of equality, but this does not invalidate the child's conception of truth and justice. The expression of compassion and empathy, which allows us to be alongside the child, is good for our spiritual growth and development as well as theirs.

In addition to these three needs of children, we also need to

Recognise that the child may have confused feelings about the abuser

This means that we need to be careful not to condemn the abuser as a person. This can apply in situations where there is no abuse as such but where parents are in conflict with each other or with other important adults in the child's life – perhaps a teacher. The child may have suffered as a consequence of adult actions, and may have confused feelings of loyalty, affection, anger and sadness. In recognising and acknowledging this confusion it is important to

Be explicit that it is not the child's fault or responsibility

The ability to convey support and unconditional acceptance of the child, and meanwhile placing responsibility on the adults in the situation, without apportioning blame, is emotionally demanding. There is biblical support for this standpoint: 'Do not judge, or you too will be judged. For in the same way as you judge others, you will be judged, and with the measure you use, it will be measured to you' (Matthew 7:1–2).

Don't sympathise with the abuser

However, a non-judgemental attitude towards the abuser as a person must neither imply the diminution of responsibility of the abuser, nor a denial of the impact of the offence against or suffering inflicted on the child. This means we must not get hooked into the cycle of abuse by becoming deflected into seeing the abuser as a victim. To that extent, don't sympathise with the abuser.

We must also *respect the time, space and process of healing*, which includes being able to *acknowledge the child's fear, anger, pain and confusion*. I now turn to look at the healing process which involves both anger and forgiveness.

7. Anger and forgiveness – helping children heal

The sexual abuse of a child arouses anger in most of us. It is this context, rather than in the literal intepretation of Jesus' words, that we can best understand what was going on for Jesus when he said, quoting again from Matthew, 'If anyone causes one of these little ones who believe in me to sin, it would be better for him to have a millstone hung around his neck and to be drowned in the depths of the sea' (Matthew 18:6). Jesus was expressing his anger at the abuse of children, even if (as Jesus was also quoted saying in the same chapter of Matthew) these things are going to happen. It is not what Jesus wants for us. Indeed, there are several occasions when Jesus expressed his anger about the way adults conducted themselves. For example, 'Jesus entered the temple area and drove out all who were buying and selling there. He overturned the tables of the money-changers and the benches of those selling doves' (Matthew 21:12).

What we need to appreciate is that anger is a positive and legitimate expression of emotion, as long as it does not become destructive. Anger can be focused and directed – for example, at those who have perpetrated abuse; but it can also be redirected – towards someone or something that has no responsibility for the cause of pain (the 'kick the cat' syndrome); or misdirected – by becoming established within a person as a fury which consumes self and others. It is this murderous anger that Jesus spoke against. Child sexual abuse is one way in which the anger of self-loathing manifests itself.

One of the more common targets of redirected anger for sexually abused children is the non-abusing parent or carer. Partly through feeling disabled or disempowered through fear to express anger at the perpetrator of the abuse, the child hits out at the easy target. But not all this anger is necessarily displaced. The child's anger may be a legitimate cry that echoes that of Jesus on the cross: 'And at the ninth hour Jesus cried out in a loud voice, "*Eloi, Eloi, lama sabachthani?*" – which means, "My God, my God, why have you forsaken me?"' (Mark 15:34).

It is not the child's responsibility for being abused. That responsibility lies directly with the abuser, and indirectly with those of us who as adults failed to care enough to protect the child from abuse, or who colluded with child care legislation that disabled and disempowered us to offer that care and love for the child, or – as I will address shortly – who failed to support and care for the perpetrator. Again this contradicts the notion of the innocent bystander and emphasises our moral imperative to stand by. I speak as a non-abusing parent who could not have prevented my children being abused, because I did not have that power. No legal system, neither in Britain nor in any other country I know of, would have supported my attempt to enforce safety for my children, which would have meant physical distance between them and their abusers, even if I had made such attempts, which I did not. That does not excuse me, but it does implicate you as well. My children needed your power, individually and collectively, to protect them.

Rightly, then, have my children been angry with me as their father for not being there for them, not protecting them, for failing to be the parent they needed, for them being abandoned by me time after time to their abuse. In that I was one of their parents, and therefore I had responsibility for their welfare and upbringing, I allowed them to be abused, even if they know rationally I did not know it was happening and I could not have done anything legally to prevent it happening.

This anger can extend outwards, to others who could or should have been there for them. I have found it hard at times that I have experienced the pain of their anger as if I was the abuser. Yet that is my abdication of responsibility, my defence, my justification that I did my best.

Maybe I did do my best. But it wasn't good enough, and the evidence for that is the fact that my children were sexually abused. So rightly they should be angry with me. Their anger is important for their emotional growth, for their ability to trust that they can be angry with me and still be loved, that there is a relationship there which is worth being angry about. And so I pray that they might be angry with God.

One of the other factors in helping children heal, a factor which is *not* advocated by Bass and Davis is forgiveness. Indeed, as I quoted them earlier, Bass and Davis see the pressure on survivors to forgive their abusers as being abusive itself. But they also acknowledge that survivors often feel stuck, desperate for healing but unable to reach the point of forgiveness.

I address anger and forgiveness again in the next chapter in terms of adult healing. At present I am focusing on the needs of the child. I consider that forgiveness is of great significance in healing for children, and that relationships may forever be fraught for survivors if they are unable to experience a sense of forgiveness. However, I am clear about the kind of forgiveness I believe to be important. It has a three-fold nature, a trinity of child, Holy Spirit and parent.

First, it is not for the survivors to crucify themselves in their attempt to forgive others. The most important first step is for them to forgive themselves, to accept themselves. It is the beginning of self-love.

Secondly, *it is to hand the forgiveness of the abuser over to a higher authority, to God*. This is exactly what Jesus did: 'Jesus said, "Father, forgive them, for they do not know what they are doing"' (Luke 23:34). Jesus did not forgive his abusers himself, he handed over that responsibility to his Father. So too must sexually abused children hand that responsibility on, for their own healing. Who do they hand it to, if they have no belief in God? Think for a moment about the implications of that for non-abusing parents and other carers, if their children hand over the responsibility of forgiveness to them. Do we deal with that ourselves? Am I to forgive my children's abusers? Or do we too pass it on? I will consider this in the next chapter.

The third aspect of forgiveness is crucial to emotional growth. It is the child's forgiveness of the non-abusing parent. It is the corollary of the anger that is so crucial to restorative relationships. The non-abusing parent is not to be seen as a secondary victim who is thereby disempowered (and therefore who the child cannot be angry at), but first as a mutual survivor and secondly as an adult who has failed to meet parental responsibilities. This releases both the child and the parent to the experience of forgiving and being forgiven. This can also be of enormous healing benefit between children who have been abused within one family, where, for example, an older abused sibling knew the abuse had moved onto a younger sibling.

One of the most powerful memories I have is of when my two children undertook this process of forgiveness. While the older sibling was not responsible for the abuse, and it was impossible for her to stop it, she still felt she had failed her brother. When the time felt right, when she had struggled with this for two years, she sought his forgiveness, expressing her sadness and compassion. He gave it, easily, readily. It gave them both hope. And yes, it gave me hope for them too.

There is of course another non-abusing parent who needs to be forgiven. This is the source of not just our emotional well-being but of our spiritual growth. The non-abusing parent who needs to be forgiven is God. Whereas the Bible emphasises the nature of God's forgiveness for us, as sinners, it is important to realise relationships are two-way. There is a legitimate anger that must be directed at God for a relationship to be restored. That anger demands attention, seeks communication, protests at the abandonment of the child. It asks to be believed that what was experienced was wrong, was abusive. It is in anger that the child says the loving parent was not good enough. It is in anger that the child says, 'Where were you? Why have you forsaken me?'

I have long been touched by the poem *Footprints*, which refers to a dream where the writer's life is represented by footprints in the sand. There are two sets of footprints, the writer's and God's. But in looking back over the lifetime of experiences, the writer noticed that at times of the greatest difficulties and sadness there was only one set of footprints.

> This really bothered me, and I questioned God about it.
>
> 'God, you said that if I decided to follow you, you would walk with me all the way. But I noticed that during the most troublesome time of my life there's only one set of footprints. I don't understand why in times when I needed you most you would leave me.'
>
> God replied, 'My precious, precious child, I love you and would never, never leave you during your times of trials and suffering. When you see only one set of footprints, it was then that I carried you.'[6]

This may well be true. But it is unlikely it always felt that way, and the child needs permission, or more often encouragement, to tell how it feels. If it feels like it was an abandonment, a betrayal of God's promise to love and care, then denying that this is the child's reality is destructive. In time, the child may feel differently about it, but the anger at God and the apology from God for the child's suffering may be the most important elements on the road to spiritual healing. The child needs God not just to say he was there, but to acknowledge that the child did not, indeed could not, know that. The child needs to know that God loves that much, and that God suffers as the child suffers, like all non-abusing parents. The child needs to hear God weeping too.

CHAPTER 9

SUPPORT STRATEGIES FOR PARENTS, CARERS AND CHURCHES

My questions

How can we protect children from being abused?
How can we support the non-abusing parents and carers of children who have been abused?
How can we help adults break out of the cycle of abuse?
Is there a positive way the churches can respond to children and adults?

In the last chapter I emphasised what justice for children means. This was:

- an acceptance of what they have experienced, and that it has been abusive;
- acknowledgement by the perpetrators of the impact of what they have done, and ideally the display of some care, concern and empathy for their victim;
- and for the abuse to stop.

I included all children affected by sexual abuse in this, not just those who would be classified as the victims of a criminal act. Therefore, siblings of abused children, or those emotionally damaged by the abuse of friends, or children whose lives have been drastically affected by the abuse perpetrated by their parents on other children, would all come into this category.

These needs are exactly the same as for children who are bullied, or who witness bullying. Children want the bully to acknowledge what has been done, to apologise for it, and not to do it again. This is the basis of restorative, healthy relationships. We all get things wrong, we do untold damage to each other, we are malicious, we have the potential to do great evil. As perpetrators we are part of the cycle of abuse. Yet adults would rather perpetuate that cycle of abuse, entering the cycle themselves as punishers, or encouraging the children who are victims to take on this role, rather than find ways to create a different kind of society, a non-abusive society.

We believe we expunge our complicity in the abuse of children by scapegoating, vilifying, punishing and eradicating abusers from our midst. Recently, energy has been expended in Canada and Britain to enforce convicted paedophiles who are released from prison to record their whereabouts with the police. The resultant campaigns to hound these people from communities is testimony not to our desire to tackle child sexual abuse at its roots but to pretend that it is perpetrated only by a very small minority of the population (almost exclusively isolated men, many with histories of being abused themselves as children). While they may pose some risk to children, they are more likely to do so in the hostile climate they attract. These vulnerable individuals take the societal wrath and scorn for child sexual abuse. Sometimes I have wondered whether those who damn loudest and campaign hardest are trying to remove their own self-doubts. Perhaps the devil within the community is too much like the devil within their own soul.

However, the hounding of known paedophiles high-lights the difficulties and failings of the external control model of response to offenders. Apart from the fact that, if we want to impose external controls on people's beha-viour, it is probably best that they live within communities where they are well known rather than anonymous, the only really effective external control to prevent a convicted paedophile from committing further child sexual abuse is permanent solitary confinement. The recent introduction of Community Protection Orders in England, whereby the police can go to court to seek a civil order restricting the movements of convicted sex offenders, is more of an attempt to reassure a fearful public rather than a realistic strategy to achieve any protection for children.

Another form of external control has arisen over the use of physical touch with children, as I discussed in Chapter 5. A reaction against the regulation of touch is the claim that adults have lost out on their spontaneity, and that there is a destruction of their innocence. Adults who have always felt comfortable with expressing physical affection to children are angry as well as anxious. Their good inten-tions are open to misinterpretation. This is wrong, they feel. It destroys relationships. While I recognise these feel-ings, I believe we need to place this the other way round. Child sexual abuse destroys a child's innocence. That is our starting point.

What I am trying to do in this book is not destroy adults' innocence but their ignorance. For it is adult ignor-ance of the child sexual abuse that is happening all around them that is the real cause of the destruction of innocence. There is a price to be paid by adults for the failings of adults, in the same way that the price of sin was loss of innocence in the garden of Eden. Because of the enormity of the child sexual abuse being perpetrated, that sin has meant that we have lost our innocence. We must grieve that. We cannot unknow what we know. As a parent of sexually abused children I have found that a dreadful experience. And I have often sought to go back and to undo the damage, to reclaim the innocence for my children and myself. But however high the price, at least I can now move forward because I have lost my ignorance. In that way I can be a more able father, and a more sensitive and aware adult to other children. It is through my loss of ignorance, rather than through my innocence, that I can gradually find an appropriate way to express physically my love for my children.

In our grief for our loss of innocence we may seek to apportion blame. But we must not implicitly put the blame onto children. It is intolerable to believe, indeed it is an example of distorted thoughts and beliefs, that if children (or adults who were abused as children) had not begun to tell we could have remained in our world of innocence. In acknowledging our sins, which we share as adults in complicity with the 'hands-on' abusers, we must be ever grateful to those who have been abused for finding the courage to tell. Indeed, we should feel a sense of privilege that they have trusted us, as adults, with the knowledge of what other adults have done. Among our other debts we owe them a debt of gratitude.

However, there is a problem in believing that the regulation of touch, an imposed external control of adult behaviour with children, will actually address the problem of child sexual abuse. To help us look at this more clearly I wish to reconsider the model, which I detailed in chapter 3, which places offender behaviour within a cycle. In particular I want to address the factors which were understood to be of significance in reducing offender behaviour (see Figure 7). Three factors were highlighted:

- a high level of arousal and desire;
- a high level of distorted beliefs and thoughts;
- a low level of internal inhibitors.

Each of these factors could be placed on a continuum, such that if one of the factors was counteracted by its opposite, eg there was only a low level of arousal and desire, then it would reduce the likelihood of offending.

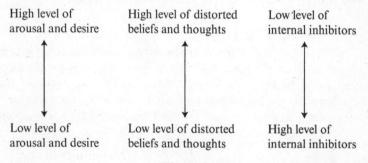

High level of arousal and desire	High level of distorted beliefs and thoughts	Low level of internal inhibitors
↕	↕	↕
Low level of arousal and desire	Low level of distorted beliefs and thoughts	High level of internal inhibitors

Figure 7

However, Wyre, who uses this model, has also proposed a number of ways in which organisations, including Church organisations, can reduce child sexual abuse offending by creating an arena of safety. This involves: creating safe places for children; having policies for safeguarding children; having someone appointed to ensure that protocols are carried out; having individuals in the organisation who know about offender behaviour; planning an organisation's work so as to minimise situations where there is a risk of abuse; ensuring staff and volunteers have clear roles; having stricter requirements and reference checks for job and volunteer applications; and so on.

All of these factors are concerned with *external controls*. Yet the history we know about child sexual abuse is that external controls are almost completely useless in preventing abuse, and even counter-productive in terms of children being able to disclose when abuse has taken place. The imposition of external controls also implies there is a righteous majority who can and will oversee a delinquent minority. We need to take heed of Jesus' concerns about the scapegoating of our peers, and consider less negative and more positive ways of addressing the issue.

The teachers of the law and the Pharisees brought in a woman caught in adultery. They made her stand before the group and said to Jesus, 'Teacher, this woman was caught in the act of adultery. In the Law Moses commanded us to stone such women. Now what do you say?' They were using this question as a trap, in order to have a basis for accusing him.

But Jesus bent down and started to write on the ground with his finger. When they kept on questioning him, he straightened up and said to them, 'If any one of you is without sin, let him be the first to throw a stone at her.' Again he stooped and wrote on the ground.

At this, those who heard began to go away one at a time, the older ones first, until only Jesus was left, with the woman still standing there. Jesus straightened up and asked her, 'Woman, where are they? Has no-one condemned you?'

'No-one, sir,' she said.

'Then neither do I condemn you,' Jesus declared. 'Go now and leave your life of sin.'

John 8:3–11

It seems obvious that we need to move away from the external control arena and enter either the arena of high level of desire and arousal, or the two arenas of distorted beliefs and thoughts, and internal inhibitors. Intervention in these arenas is much harder to implement, in that we are not able to package beliefs, inhibitions or desires in neatly ordered and detached regulations of behaviour, with social rewards for compliance and sanctions for non-compliance.

It is at our core that we find both the source of distorted beliefs and thoughts and our lack of internal inhibitors – in our self-loathing. To overcome our self-loathing requires us to enter deeply and spiritually into relationships with each other: to eschew bystanding and resolve to stand by each other, to recognise our inter-connectedness, and to establish our compassion and empathy which is a necessary part of our healing, our therapy.

At one level I consider that what has led to our self-loathing is irrelevant. This is not to deny the particular experiences, the type of abuse that may have been inflicted, or the unique history of our fellow beings which has led to self-loathing. Rather, it is to acknowledge and accept that we need to address whatever has led us to loathe ourselves, and that it is only by sharing a commitment to each other's social, emotional and spiritual welfare – to begin to love ourselves and each other – that we can resolve issues and find the care and support that will help us refrain from reverting to destructive patterns. The relationships we have or can establish are the most crucial determinants of our ability to recover from self-loathing.

I quote from Alice Miller again:

It greatly aids the success of therapeutic work when we become aware of our parents' destructive patterns at work within us. But to free ourselves from these patterns we need more than an intellectual awareness: we need an emotional confrontation with our parents in an inner dialogue.[1]

Part of the process of confronting our destructive patterns is to express our anger. However, it is important to differentiate between legitimate anger and the illegitimate hatred which is our repressed horror, so displaced that it can lead us to scapegoat others and abuse vulnerable people. It 'poisons and blinds the soul, devours the memory and the mind, and kills the capacity for compassion and insight'.[2]

Legitimate anger releases us from the tensions and restraints of repressed horrors. Miller believes it is crucial to our growth

above all because it opens our eyes to reality (both past and present) and frees us from lies and illusions . . . It is therefore empowering . . . We will have a new capacity to identify cruelty and injustice, and to speak out and fight against it.[3]

It is also through redressing our self-loathing that we, through the love of our neighbours, can each find our hope of salvation. Jesus told us that the first commandment was to love God, and the second was to 'love your neighbour as yourself' (Matthew 22:39). He didn't say it was easy.

But I don't know whether I can do this, for two reasons. First, all the time I am full of self-loathing what sense can I make of loving someone else as myself? Clearly, and particularly so if I abuse others, I am demonstrating that edict, but not at all in the way it was intended. In other words, I am failing to love others in the way I fail to love myself. Secondly, what if my neighbour, perhaps even in the literal sense, is a convicted child abuser? Not only have I to consider what my children have experienced at the hands of abusers, I also happen to have an abuser next door.

Jesus made other statements that link closely with loving your neighbour: 'Do not judge, and you will not be judged. Do not condemn, and you will not be condemned. Forgive, and you will be forgiven' (Luke 6:37). 'But I tell you: Love your enemies and pray for those who persecute you' (Matthew 5:44). 'Forgive us our sins, for we also forgive everyone who sins against us' (Luke 11:4). I have again deliberately juxtaposed anger and forgiveness, as both are essentially enmeshed. Loving our neighbours, and loving our enemies, may seem a noble and indeed desirable idea – until we are confronted with it. Then anger and forgiveness arise not as concepts but as a struggle within our thoughts, beliefs, emotions and acts of will. It is easier to return to the cycle of abuse, and to feel and act punitively or indifferently.

Corrie Ten Boom's experience powerfully illustrates this reality. Corrie had been involved in the Dutch Resistance, and had been imprisoned by the Nazis at Ravensbruck. Two years after the war ended, she was spreading the message that God forgives at meetings around Germany. At one meeting, having given her talk, a man approached her. She suddenly recognised him as a guard who had been at Ravensbruck, and struggled not to visualise him again in his uniform and with his leather crop. Her blood froze. He had contributed to her own degradation and to the death of her sister in the concentration camp. He did not recognise her. He had approached her to congratulate her on the message she had given regarding God's forgiveness of sins. He wanted to shake her hand. And, as she had mentioned her experiences at Ravensbruck and as he had been a guard there, he wanted her to forgive him.

Betsie had died in that place – could he erase her slow terrible death simply for the asking?

It could not have been many seconds that he stood there, hand held out, but to me it seemed hours as I wrestled with the most difficult thing I had ever had to do.

For I had to do it – I knew that. The message that God forgives has a prior condition: that we forgive those who have injured us. 'If you do not forgive men their trespasses,' Jesus says, 'neither will your Father in heaven forgive your trespasses.'

I knew it not only as a commandment of God, but as a daily experience. Since the end of the war I had had a home in Holland for victims of Nazi brutality. Those who were able to forgive their enemies were also able to return to the outside world and rebuild their lives, no matter what the physical scars. Those who nursed bitterness remained invalids. It was as simple and as horrible as that.

And still I stood there with the coldness clutching my heart. But forgiveness is not an emotion – I knew that. Forgiveness is an act of the will, and the will can function regardless of the temperature of the heart. 'Jesus, help me!' I prayed silently. 'I can lift the hand. I can do that much. You supply the feeling.'

And so woodenly, mechanically, I thrust my hand into the one stretched out to me. And as I did, an incredible thing took place. The current started in my shoulder, raced down my arm, sprang into our joined hands. And then this healing warmth seemed to flood my whole being, bringing tears to my eyes.

'I forgive you brother!' I cried. 'With all my heart!' For a long moment we grasped each other's hands, the former guard and the former prisoner. I had never known God's love so intensely as I did then.[4]

The act of forgiveness dissipates the anger and bitterness that has built up and been nurtured. My anger at what my children have experienced is, I believe, legitimate. It is not misplaced or misdirected. I am angry that a number of adults freely chose to abuse them, and then chose to deny that this had happened. I am angry that they have denied the pain and suffering that has so affected their lives. And I don't want to forgive them. I recognise that I have believed and felt it would be a betrayal of my children to forgive their abusers. But maybe I'm wrong. There is a fundamental difference between forgiveness and minimising; between forgiving and forgetting; between forgiveness and trust; and between forgiveness and reconciliation (although forgiveness opens up that possibility).

But the issue is this: for my children to heal, and for me to heal, we need to be able to release our anger, and erase our bitterness. We need to forgive for our spiritual growth. Moreover, if my children hand over to me the burden of forgiveness, as their non-abusing parent, as it is more than they can reasonably manage and it is part of my parental responsibilities, or if they seek support from me in the same way that Corrie Ten Boom sought the help of God, what am I doing to them by refusing to take on this burden? Face to face with the need to forgive, I tell myself I can't do it. It is beyond me. But is that my anger with God, challenging him, defying him? But at whose cost?

I want us all to recover from the abuse. For me, healing and spiritual growth are the ultimate outcomes that I want from this process of suffering. I want to be freed from this deadening burden. So I need to make sense of forgiveness.

First, if one or more of the abusers unexpectedly came to my door and demanded forgiveness, I would not give it. I can picture this scene, and I would interpret it as a further form of persecution. In other words, I would see it as a continuation of a power game, inviting me to become the victim. I can visualise the smirks, the implicit ridicule. It hits me as a further invasion, another abuse, taking something from me and my children rather than giving anything back. I would, as is apparent, doubt their sincerity. There would have to be preconditions met to convince me that forgiveness was genuinely requested, and that I could offer it sincerely.

Secondly, the conditions for me to feel able to engage in forgiveness would include an absolute and unequivocal acknowledgement that they had perpetrated sexual abuse on my children. A full recognition of the facts and experiences, the suffering inflicted, would have to be made. This would involve them taking full responsibility for these actions, without deflecting culpability onto others. The next condition would be the full repentance of the actions, which would include an apology for the abuse inflicted.

Thirdly, if these conditions were met I would not feel a need for reparation or reconciliation. Nor would I feel a need for punishment. I would not want to enter discussions about trust and future behaviour. These are issues for the abusers, not essentially for me. My forgiveness does not absolve them of responsibility, it confirms it, but then lays it to rest. It does not pretend that nothing has happened. It does not pretend that they will now refrain from abusing other children.

Fourthly, I would not want them exposed to my children again unless my children were absolutely sure that this is what they wanted, and that they had ensured their safety – physical, emotional and spiritual – in any situation where there may be contact.

Fifthly, and of central importance to my healing, I need the support of fellow humans as well as God if I am to forgive. Unlike Corrie Ten Boom, I'm not sure I can make it with God alone. Maybe that says something about the lack of strength I have in my faith. If so, then it is good that I acknowledge it. Just now I need the support of fellow adults.

Sixthly, what happens if the abusers do not come knocking at my door seeking forgiveness? As it is, I don't know where they live (although I could find them if I really wanted to). Does that mean I am exonerated from the responsibility to forgive? Or can I forgive unilaterally, in the absence of their acknowlegement of their abuse and their declarations of repentence, and in their physical absence? It seems to me that there is a selfish element to forgiveness, a legitimate caring of the self which is part of healing. To forgive is to move on; to forgive is to release the power the abuser may have over us; to forgive is to free ourselves to be more than just survivors of abuse – we free ourselves to become fuller people; we free ourselves to love ourselves.

If forgiveness is the act of spiritual healing, it is possible to regard self-loathing as the locus of evil. Evil, then, exists as a potential within us – all of us – that requires a spiritual relationship with God to transend. We are indeed, as Corrie Ten Boom stated, nearer to God in that act of forgiveness, of healing our self-loathing.

But what do we do about the abusers? Whether or not they seek forgiveness, we have a problem of major proportions, given the statistical evidence for the number of children who are abused. Abusers are everywhere. Are we able to help them heal? Does this compromise our need to help children and their non-abusing parents and carers to heal? In particular, how do we as Christian adults respond?

First, it seems we have to break the silence about abuse: to 'normalise' it, as I said earlier. This means we have to remove the privilege of confidentiality. Within a culture that places child sexual abuse within a criminal justice system, there is less likelihood that abusers will disclose what they are doing and seek help. This is evidenced in the telephone calls to Childline in Britain, where abusers desperately want help but fear the consequences of giving their names and addresses. No names, no punishment; but no help either. Moreover, if the cost of confession is confidentiality, then the person receiving the confession is implicated in the abuse.

This has been a not infrequent problem within the Church. Parkinson[5] argues hypothetically that it might be possible to persuade a father who is sexually abusing his daughter to break the secrecy by appealing to the following motives: the abuse will be uncovered sooner or later; prosecutions can take place years later, so a lapse of time will not resolve matters; openness will provide a better chance of getting skilled therapy; admission is an act of loving; and it might make a relationship viable between him and his daughter at some future date.

I find his arguments unconvincing, as I'm sure most abusers and survivors would too. It is only in a climate where child sexual abuse does not involve the criminal justice system that the shift from confidentiality can be constructively undertaken. In my case, because none of my children's abusers have been convicted, none of them can be named. Indeed, if I made it obvious who they were, even without naming them, I might be liable to legal retribution through the civil court in terms of libel.

We need to create a climate where both the act and the perpetrators can be named. At present the act and the victims carry the shame. That is unjust. Shame itself is destructive. Naming does not have to mean shaming, either for the victims or the abusers. Despite the current media and public hounding of convicted paedophiles, as mentioned earlier, there is general consensus among the police and social work agencies that this is a major distraction from the real issues, it compounds the secrecy, and hides the failings of social and legal systems to address the enormity and complexity of everyday child sexual abuse in society.

If familial abusers in particular were able to be more open about their actions, without fear of major reprisals, punishment or retribution, it would provide much more scope to reduce the incidence of offending and allow us to intervene positively: acknowledging, protecting, preventing, helping, supporting, loving. Abusers could begin to address the factors that have led to them abusing children, and we could offer support to their victims.

The response by some churches to disclosures of abusing has been to perceive the abuser as being spiritually or morally deficient, and the solution is simply that they need to find or regain a true relationship with God. While there are arguments against this spiritualising of the problem, at one level it is appropriate. For those who loathe themselves, finding a sense of God's love is an important element of healing, and in particular spiritual healing.

However, the danger is that this is seen as simplistic and, effectively, miraculous. For an offender to receive a cathartic conversion, and overnight to transform from a perpetrator of child sexual abuse into a devout and moral adult whose offences are in the past, is at best naive. It is a sign that the Church wants to magic the problem away, and has found a neat and theologically convenient way of doing it. What we do know is that for those with a lifetime based on abusive experiences, both as victim and as perpetrator, it may never be possible for them to eradicate permanently the factors (such as motivation, arousal and desire, and lack of internal inhibitors) that allow them to abuse. Moreover, the cycle of abuse may be indelibly imprinted within their thoughts, beliefs, feelings and actions.

Churches are not doing the abusers any favours by colluding with a pretence that all is well. Some churches have allowed and encouraged abusers who have repented to work with children in youth groups, Sunday schools and similar ventures. Apart from setting abusers up to fail, and thereby children up to be abused, the motivation behind this is spurious. It seems that there is a failure to acknowledge that excessive exposure to temptation is neither an intrinsically necessary part of spiritual growth nor of recovery from patterns of abuse.

Churches do need to be prepared for disclosures of abuse suffered and perpetrated. Indeed, part of the preparation is to acknowledge that child sexual abuse takes place within the clergy and families of all church denominations. No single church is likely to be unaffected by it, even though there may be ignorance that the abuse is being perpetrated.

> Churches ought to be in the front line of prevention work, not only because they have a God-given mandate to stand up against evil, but because they are so vulnerable to the problem of sexual abuse. Churches have an extensive involvement in work with children and young people . . . The church is therefore a community which is likely to attract people with a sexual interest in children.[6]

Parkinson recommends that there is more openness about sexuality within Christian communities, and that there are educational programmes about the nature and extent of child sexual abuse. He also proposes raising the value of children and of ministry to children. Children are not added extras, or valuable only as potential adults. His other strategies are along the lines of external controls, similar to those advocated by Wyre, and which I find less convincing.

However, one of the ways of naming and claiming abuse, 'normalising' both those who are abused and their abusive experiences, is to help survivors of abuse to develop their ministry. An argument is put forward by Hancock and Mains that those who have experienced healing from their experiences may have the compassion and empathy to offer to share their journey with others.

> As the extent of the problem of child abuse becomes generally known, we must realise that there are simply not enough professional or pastoral counsellors to go around. People will have to minister to each other, sharing with the next person the comfort they have received in their distress.[7]

This is not second-rate counselling or ministry. It is explicitly acknowledging that abuse is an everyday occurrence, and that (however devastating) healing is possible. It empowers those who have suffered to recover together, which produces the potential for both enlightenment – to expose reality – and for transforming reality. This can be done at an institutional level – for example, by encouraging those who have experienced abuse to help develop the conscience of the Church, both to address the needs of adults who are potential abusers and to support survivors of abuse, and their parents, carers and friends.

However, it is important that the burden of responsibility is not shifted onto survivors of abuse alone. The more we wish to harness their knowledge and skills, the more everyone else needs to support them to do this. Moreover, it is only in the past decade or so that survivors have been offered resources to any significant degree that validate their experiences, and one of the features of abuse is to isolate victims from each other. It requires a major act of trust for one abuse victim to feel able to share experiences with another – it must not be assumed that there is a 'natural grouping' of those who have experienced abuse.

It is the support of others for my healing and my children's healing that I wish now to address. One of the guide-lines for supporting survivors of sexual abuse is to *find supports for yourself – the healing process will take its toll on you too.* What an understatement!

For me to be able to heal, to erase my self-loathing, to recover from my secondary abuse as the non-abusing parent, I need to feel the strength of consistent loving adults. I must not seek that from my children – it is not their responsibility to care for me. I do not need to be victimised or rescued; nor do I need to be punished for what has happened to my children. Like most non-abusing parents, I have already crucified myself with feelings of guilt for what my children experienced. I do not need to run the gauntlet of suspicion and distrust, or endure aloofness and indifference.

The disclosure of abuse by my children and the attendant investigations and criminal and civil court processes took an enormous toll. We were fighting, literally, for my children's lives. My partner, who is now my children's stepmother, dedicated her time, commitment and energy to their survival. This went on for years, and still does to a lesser degree – eight years since the abuse was first disclosed. Meanwhile, many of our friends and acquaintances became scarce. To be fair, we must have been extremely distressing companions for them. Also, who knows what our experiences raised in them, particularly for our female friends who undoubtedly struggled with the accounts of women sexual abusers.

I am not suggesting all our friends deserted us – far from it. But at a time when we needed more care, love and support, and when we had less to give them in return, we found it harder to find friends. We needed unconditional love, care and support. We needed acceptance, and hope.

Looking back, it was an excruciatingly difficult time. It is almost impossible to know how my wife and I survived, as adults let alone parents. The human cost over the years has been beyond our understanding; certainly it fundamentally affected our self-belief and our souls. It affected every member of our family. During the court case the advocate for the prime abuser appeared to set out to destroy me as a person. According to my advocate, that was his explicit purpose, and the outcome after I had been subjected to four and a half horrific days of ridicule, intrusive interrogation and vilification was, that nothing had been lost or gained – we were no worse off than before we had started.

We have experienced self-loathing. We found counsellors and therapists who supported us as adults, but we struggled to find professional help for the children. Those professionals who were used to help the children were in some cases destructive, and added to the system abuse. Our inability to offer the children absolute protection in the future racked us. We needed adults who could reach out to the children, to care, support and accept them. Again we were disappointed. There were few adults who were able to do this.

We were surrounded by professionals and members of the community who took on hostile roles within the cycle of abuse, as well as those who were bystanders. In our goldfish bowl, we were watched. But we were not seen as we were, as fellow humans in distress. We screamed, we cried, we despaired – but so few people could cope. They walked by on the other side.

APOCALYPSE NOW: BEYOND SURVIVAL

Whereas I earlier stated that fear eats the soul, child sexual abuse murders it. I recall seeing the film *Apocalypse Now* in the late 1970s. I only saw it once, but it had a big impact on me. I wrote an article about the implications raised by the film for how we conducted ourselves in society. The essence for me was that the hero of the film, an American army lieutenant, could not cope with the normality of peace. He was insane in that setting. He voluteered to return to Vietnam on a special mission. There he became, or appeared, well adjusted. He was only normal in an abnormal context.

His object of the mission was to destroy Kurtz, of whom it was said 'he dead'. Kurtz was insane, yet it was his environment that had brought about this madness. In a non-abusive environment he would have been different. Then there was the crazy major who played the 'Ride of the Valkyries' from his helicopter as he bombed and blasted villages. He was insane in any environment.

We live in an insane world, insanity being the manifestation of self-loathing, a world in which so many of our children are subjected to sexual abuse. Our apocalypse –

literally our revelation that we can overcome it – is in front of us. It is now. Are we to continue in apparent normality in this insane world? Are we to allow the insane world to destroy us? Are we too crazy to do anything sensible?

Our apocalypse can harness the spiritual power to create a different world on earth. In his remarkable book, Holloway encourages us to recognise that our given understanding of the way the world is, and the way we are, are not irrevocable certainties. Truth is still to be attained.

> This is why making ourselves disciples of truth also involves the discipline of contemplation. We have to look steadily and without fear at the new reailty that confronts us, knowing it could be a gift from the God who is already ahead of us.[1]

The right and ability of children to live without abuse, and to develop their spirituality, is of major importance if we are to take our spiritual journey seriously. I have pointed out some of the ways we can overcome abuse and begin to heal. For example, decriminalising child sexual abuse is liberating for children and adults. It removes system abuse; it increases the opportunities for abusers to seek help; it increases the opportunities for children to tell the truth about abuse and be heard; it helps break the cycle of abuse; and it fundamentally interrupts bystander patterns.

Revising the civil and private laws which give rights to adults precedence over responsibilities to our children, and which enshrine the notion that biology is more important than love, is also of paramount importance.

We have both a moral imperative and a moral justification to support these changes. Holloway argues:

> This is something that the new familial fundamentalism refuses to acknowledge. It cleaves to the single paradigm or

template theory of human relationships, claiming that there is only one correct way of organising ourselves and our sexual and family relationships. This is essentially an abstract approach to reality that simply refuses to acknowledge the historical or political nature of human experience. Its static perfectionism is the enemy not only of ordinary human happiness but of the genius of Jesus, which was passionate in its advocacy of human need over all system and law.[2]

No longer can we pretend that child sexual abuse is a problem for 'the authorities' to deal with. It is our problem, everybody's business. Our objective as a society has to be beyond doing least harm. Harm reduction models are defeatist: in effect they say we cannot prevent whole-scale abuse from happening, but maybe we can slow it down a little. Tinkering with the issues at the margin colludes with abuse and creates more victims.

We need to move beyond helping victims become survivors. If we have a purpose in our existence it must be more than wearing a badge at the end of our days which says 'I survived'. We need to create the conditions under which we can hold ourselves upright and say that, whatever the hardships and whatever our imperfections, 'I truly live'.

Two Christian practices are central to this new paradigm, if expanded and realised in their full potential. The first is peace and the second communion. The cessation of abuse is like the cessation of any conflict: it is an essential prerequisite for peace but it is not peace. Peace is deeper and has a more spiritual than physical nature. Peace is a central tenet of Christianity and it is through the painful process of achieving the peace (which is God's gracious gift, beyond our understanding) that we must strive. Likewise, communion is more than the practice of partaking in the Eucharist. It equalises us all, abolishes our false divisions, and helps us to become whole as people. As we partake physically, we experience our spiritual inter-connectedness. We too are one with God.

Both peace and communion call us to a life of commitment to love ourselves and each other, to a practical ministry. We are all our children's parents. We are each other's therapists, each other's carers and supporters. We are each other's advocates, and celebrants of our achievements.

One of the celebrations we require is to confirm our spiritual renewal, as survivors of abuse, as survivors of secondary abuse, as survivors of tertiary abuse. We need our rites of passage, to acknowledge first that we have survived but that there is further growth ahead, there are new rites of passage towards which we strive. There will be many occasions when we are reminded of the abuse we have suffered, or (as non-abusing parents) of the sufferings of our children. As we revisit these times, we need to confirm that they are past, and celebrate again. Healing is not an event, it is a continuous process. It is a loving process.

In the growth of love, which is our spiritual commitment to ourselves and to others, and our promise from God, we give and receive care, support and ministry; in so doing we reach beyond survival.

The practices of peace and communion, and the celebration of the rites of passage, are central to our spiritual growth. But our healing as individuals also has to come from deep within each of us. The survival strategies may have helped us stay alive; perhaps they have ensured that we are still making a journey. Moving beyond survival is scary. We may have received skilled help as a victim or as a non-abusing parent. We may have expressed great anger. We may have considered forgiveness for our abusers. We may have felt the boundless love of a partner (as in my case). All these have helped us to reach the point on our journey where we have to go alone. Alone to God, and thereby with God. We have to make the apocalyptic leap of faith so that we can cross the void where we shed the survival strategies, where we can unlock our armour, expose our heart and soul, and take the ultimate risk of being betrayed again.

I wrote earlier that it seems to me that there is a selfish element to forgiveness, a legitimate caring of the self which is part of healing. To forgive is to move on; to forgive is to release the power the abuser may have over us; to forgive is to free ourselves to be more than just survivors of abuse. We free ourselves to become fuller people; we free ourselves to love ourselves.

Part of the forgiveness required is the forgiveness of self. As a non-abusing parent I had to reach the point of forgiving myself for what happened to my children. I had to forgive myself in order to stop loathing myself. I had to free myself from my survival strategies and open myself to being hurt badly again. I had to make my leap of faith. I wanted to restore fully my relationships with my wife and with all our children. One of my children I had greater difficulties with, and I knew if I could make that leap with him, to give him my heart and soul, then I would be healed.

I have stood on the edge of the abyss so many times. My being has been torn in two, partly wanting to move on, partly steadfastly holding on, however destructive I knew that to be. Terrified. This damaged me as much as it did those who needed me to move on. But I had to do it alone, they could not carry me. And I could not do it. I could not even admit what it was I could not do.

And then one day, when I was not expecting it, the moment came which I knew would change my life. I had to go. In certain respects it was more terrifying than I had ever envisaged, but the more I allowed myself to enter the fear the more it dissipated. I went over the abyss, but I did not fall. Instead, I rose higher and lighter, as all my baggage tumbled away, my bitterness, my defensiveness, my need to hold onto my perfect image, my need to impress. My faith was enough.

Instead, I could acknowledge my failings, laugh at my foibles, feel my energy, hold my children again, and I could express fully the love I had always felt for them and for my wife. I was strong. I was whole. The abuse was in the past, and so for ever was the part of me that needed to be cast off too.

The words of Martin Luther King resounded through me: 'Free at last, free at last, Oh my God, free at last.'

The place beyond survival is exhilarating. But it is real, and in reality difficulties continue to exist. It is not a false dawn; it is not sweetness and light. The test for those who have reached beyond survival comes when there is a significant relationship crisis to cope with. It can focus on a core aspect of the personality, or involve ridiculing a sensitive feature of the body. It can be a breach of commitment or a betrayal of love.

I found my test, of major proportions, coming within a few hours of making my leap of faith. It shocked me to my new foundations – the second major life change in less than a day. How easily I could have gone back across the abyss, picking up as many bits of baggage as I could retrieve. I did not. I will not. However hard life is, I didn't reach the end of my journey just to scamper back wounded. As I quoted Richard Holloway above, 'We have to look steadily and without fear at the new reality that confronts us, knowing it could be a gift from the God who is already ahead of us.'

But that's a new journey.

NOTES

Introduction: Child sexual abuse and Christianity

1. Browning, E.B., 'The cry of the children' in Graham, C., ed., *Elizabeth Barrett Browning. Selected Poems* (Everyman: London, 1996), p. 165.
2. *Ibid.*

Chapter 1: Children suffering: The incidence and impact of child sexual abuse

1. Moorehead, C., quoted by Spencer, D., in 'Pressure group slams "sham" of a charter' in *Times Educational Supplement* (London: 1997), p. 8.
2. Campbell, B., *Unofficial Secrets* (Virago: London, 1988).
3. Bass, E. and Davis, L., *The Courage to Heal* (Cedar: London, 1996), p. 20.
4. Campbell, B., *op. cit.*, p. 4.
5. See Brown, K., *To Bully No More – The Pupil Pack* (St Andrew's College: Glasgow, 1994); and Brown, K., *Bullying – What Can Parents Do?* (Monarch: Crowborough, 1997).
6. See Haller, K.C., 'A clinical sample of women who have sexually abused children' in *Journal of Child Sexual Abuse* 4 (3), 1995, pp. 13–31.

7. Mendel, M.P., *The Male Survivor. The Impact of Sexual Abuse* (Sage Publications: London, 1995), p. 21.
8. *Ibid.*, p. 22.
9. Renvoize, J., *Innocence Destroyed. A Study of Child Sexual Abuse* (Routledge: London, 1993), pp. 116–117.
10. Miller, A., *The Drama of Being a Child* (Virago: London, 1995), p. 97.
11. Young, V., 'Women abusers – a feminist view' in Elliott, M., *Female Sexual Abuse of Children: The Ultimate Taboo* (Longman: Harlow, 1993), pp. 114–115.
12. Quoted in Morton, T., 'Going behind the satanic mask' in *The Scotsman* (Edinburgh: 3 June 1997), p. 6.
13. Quoted by Mitchell, D., 'Conference hears calls to end silence on abuse' in *Community Care* no. 1181 (17–23 July 1997), p. 3.
14. Mendel, M.P., *op. cit.*, p. 34.

Chapter 2: Recognising the signs

1. Lew, M., *Victims No Longer. Men Recovering from Incest and Other Child Sexual Abuse* (Cedar: London, 1993).
2. NCH Action for Children, *Hearing the Truth* (NCH: London, 1996).
3. Miller, A., *op. cit.*, p. 24.
4. Bass, E. and Davis, L., *op. cit.*, p. 22.
5. *Ibid.*, their italics.
6. Bloom, S., quoted in *Journal of Psycho-history*, *21* (4) (Spring 1994).
7. Lew, M., *op. cit.*, p. 120.
8. Research evidence reviewed by O'Grady, C., 'Secrets made to be broken' in *Times Educational Supplement 2* (Edinburgh: 23 May 1997).

Chapter 3: The cycle of sexual abuse

1. Williams, L.M. and Finkelhor, D., 'The characteristics of incestuous fathers' in Marshall, W.L., Laws, D.R. and

Barbaree, H.E., eds, *Handbook of Sexual Assault: Issues, Theories and Treatment of the Offender* (Plenum: New York, 1990).

2. Miller, A., *Thou Shalt Not Be Aware* (Pluto Press: London, 1985), p. 6.

3. Brown, K., (1997) *op. cit.*, p. 45.

4. *Ibid.*, p. 76.

5. See for example Dobash, R.P., Carnie, J. and Waterhouse, L. 'Child Sexual Abusers. Recognition and Response' in Waterhouse, L., ed., *Child Abuse and Child Abusers. Protection and Prevention* (Jessica Kingsley: London, 1996), pp. 113–135; and Browne, K. and Herbert, M., *Preventing Family Violence* (John Wiley: Chichester, 1997), esp. pp. 246–260.

6. Allardyce, J., 'Fears over child self-mutilation' in *The Scotsman* (Edinburgh: 26 November 1997), p. 9.

7. Browne, K. and Herbert, M., *op. cit.*, p. 248.

8. McCann, I.L., Sakheim, D.K. and Abrahamson, D.J., 'Trauma and victimisation: a model of psychological adaptation' in *The Counselling Psychologist 16* (4) (1988), pp. 531–594.

9. Brown, K., (1997) *op. cit.*

10. For the Drama Triangle, see Karpman, S., 'Fairy tales and script drama analysis' in *Transactional Analysis Bulletin 7* (26) (1968), pp. 39–43. For the bystander role, see Clarkson, P., *The Bystander (An End to Innocence in Human Relationships?)* (Whurr Publishers: London, 1996).

11. Brown, K., (1997) *op. cit.*, pp. 74–75.

12. Sinason, V., *Mental Handicap and the Human Condition. New Approaches from the Tavistock* (Free Association Books: London, 1992), p. 139.

13. Norwood, R., *Women Who Love Too Much* (Arrow Books: London, 1986).

Chapter 4: The problem of justice

1. National Commission of Inquiry into the Prevention of Child Abuse, *Childhood Matters* (NSPCC: London, 1996).

2. Siddall, R., 'Damage limitation' in *Community Care* no. 1195 (23–29 October 1997), p. 24.

3. Moran, E., Gillies, J., Mayes, G. and MacLeod, L., *An Evaluation of a Children's Safety Training Programme* (SOED, SHHD, SHEG and ESRC: Edinburgh, 1990).

4. La Fontaine, J.S., *Child Sexual Abuse* (Polity Press: Cambridge, 1990), p. 77.

5. Miles, R., *The Children We Deserve* (Harper Collins: London, 1994), p. 165.

6. MacLeod, M., *Child Protection: Everybody's Business* (Childline/Community Care: Sutton, 1997), p. 4.

7. Thompson, A., 'Common convictions' in *Community Care* no. 1137 (12–18 September 1996), p. 14.

Chapter 5: Fears and anxieties – the problem for adults

1. AHTS guidance quoted in Munro, N., 'Never be alone with a pupil' in *Times Educational Supplement Scotland* (Edinburgh: 14 November 1997), p. 1.

2. Eaton, L., 'To hug or not to hug' in *Community Care* no. 1189 (11–17 September 1997).

3. Quigley, E., 'Innocence lost ahead of time' in *Scotland on Sunday* (Edinburgh: 3 May 1996), p. 14.

4. Penn, H. and McQuail, S., *Childcare as a Gendered Occupation* (DFEE Research Series no. 23: London, 1997).

5. Quoted in Sierz, A., 'Beyond good and evil' in *Times Educational Supplement 2* (Edinburgh: 31 January 1997), p. 6.

6. See Aries, P., *Centuries of Childhood* (Penguin: Harmondsworth, 1973).

7. Quoted in MacKinnon, S., 'Off the streets' in *Times Educational Supplement 2* (Edinburgh: 14 November 1997), p. 3.

8. Campbell, B., *op. cit.*, p. 69.

9. Brown, K., (1994), *op cit*.

10. Clarkson, P., *op. cit.*

Chapter 6: Coping with disclosures

1. 'Kerry', a survivor of child sexual abuse, quoted in the review of *No Child of Mine*, a Meridian TV drama documentary based on her experiences.
2. Miles, R., *op. cit.*, p. 165.
3. The Children's Society, *Child Prostitution in Britain* (1997).
4. Quoted in Young, S., 'Charity asks schools to protect child prostitutes' in *Times Educational Supplement* (London: 7 March 1997), p. 12.
5. Sinason, V., *op. cit.*, Chapter 6.
6. Adapted from Bass, E. and Davis, L., *op. cit.*
7. Finkelhor, D., Hotaling, G., Lewis, I.A. and Smith, C., 'Sexual abuse in a national survey of adult men and women: prevalence, characteristics, and risk factors' in *Child Abuse and Neglect 14* (1990), pp. 19–28.
8. Clarkson, P., *op. cit.*, p. 21.

Chapter 7: The filth and the faith – where does God fit in?

1. See Adams, M.M. and Adams, R.M., eds, *The Problem of Evil* (Oxford University Press: Oxford, 1990), p. 2.
2. It is now accepted that the author was unlikely to be Matthew the tax-gatherer who followed Jesus, but a Jewish Christian who followed in Matthew's footsteps in the new Church.
3. Sharrock, D., 'Paedophile priest jailed for twelve years' in *The Guardian* (London: 26 July 1997), p. 2.
4. Coles, J., '£73m award against cleric' in *The Guardian* (London: 26 July 1997), p. 2.
5. Forrest, T., 'Bishop to address home abuse issue' in *Press and Journal* (Aberdeen: 13 June 1997), p. 9.
6. Urquhart, F., 'Nuns accused of child torture hit back at accusers' in *The Scotsman* (Edinburgh: 29 January 1998).
7. Parkinson, P., *Child Sexual Abuse and the Churches* (Hodder and Stoughton: London, 1997), p. 30.

8. Holloway, R., *Dancing on the Edge* (Fount: London, 1997), pp. 126–127.
9. Bass, E. and Davis, L., *op. cit.*, p. 150.
10. Browning, E.B., *op. cit.*, p. 170.

Chapter 8: Revelations

1. Miller, A., *Banished Knowledge* (Virago: London, 1997), p. 5.
2. Mathieson, T., *The Politics of Abolition* (Scandinavian Studies in Criminology, vol. 4, 1974).
3. Clarkson, P., *op. cit.*, p. 34.
4. Peck, M.S., *The Road Less Travelled. A New Psychology of Love, Traditional Values and Spiritual Growth* (Rider: London, 1988), p. 81.
5. Miller, A., (1995) *op. cit.*, pp. 96–97.
6. Anon., *Footprints*.

Chapter 9: Support strategies for parents, carers and churches

1. Miller, A., (1995) *op. cit.*, p. 135.
2. *Ibid.*, p. 137.
3. *Ibid.*
4. Boom, C.T., originally quoted in *Guidepost Magazine* (Guildposts Assoc. Inc., 1972); here quoted in Gumbel, N., *Challenging Lifestyle* (Kingsway Publications: Eastbourne, 1996), pp. 63–64.
5. Parkinson, P., *op cit.*, p. 195.
6. *Ibid.*, p. 255.
7. Hancock, M. and Mains, K.B., *Child Sexual Abuse. A Hope for Healing* (Highland: Guildford, 1987), p. 171.

Afterword: Apocalypse now: beyond survival

1. Holloway, R., *op. cit.*, p. 195.
2. *Ibid.*, p. 171.

BIBLIOGRAPHY

Adams, M.M. and Adams, R.M., eds *The Problem of Evil* (Oxford University Press: Oxford, 1990).

Aries, P., *Centuries of Childhood* (Penguin: Harmondsworth, 1973).

Bass, E. and Davis, L., *The Courage to Heal* (Cedar: London, 1996).

Batty, D., ed., *Sexually Abused Children: Making Their Placements Work* (BAAF: London, 1991).

Bray, M., *Poppies on the Rubbish Heap. Sexual Abuse – The Child's Voice* (Canongate: Edinburgh, 1991).

Brown, K., *To Bully No More – The Pupil Pack* (St Andrews College: Glasgow, 1994).

Brown, K., *Bullying – What Can Parents Do?* (Monarch: Crowborough, 1997).

Brown, K., 'Child protection: beyond repair' in *Professional Social Work* (BASW: Birmingham, 1997).

Browne, K. and Herbert, M., *Preventing Family Violence* (John Wiley: Chichester, 1997).

Campbell, B., *Unofficial Secrets. Child Sexual Abuse – The Cleveland Case* (Virago Press: London, 1988).

Cashman, H., *Christianity and Child Sexual Abuse* (SPCK: London, 1993).

Clarkson, P., *The Bystander (An End to Innocence in Human Relationships?)* (Whurr Publishers: London, 1996).

Coles, R., *The Moral Intelligence of Children* (Bloomsbury: London, 1997).

Davis, L., *The Courage to Heal Workbook* (Harper and Row: New York, 1990).

Elliot, M., *Female Sexual Abuse of Children: The Ultimate Taboo* (Longman: Harlow, 1993).

Farmer, E. and Owen, M., *Child Protection Practice: Private Risks and Public Remedies* (HMSO: London, 1995).

Flaherty, S.M., *Woman, Why Do You Weep? Spirituality for Survivors of Childhood Sexual Abuse* (Paulist Press: New Jersey, 1992).

Forward, S. and Buck, C., *Betrayal of Innocence. Incest and its Devastation* (Penguin: Harmondsworth, 1981).

Gill, M., *Free to Love. Sexuality and Pastoral Care* (HarperCollins: London, 1994).

Goleman, D., *Emotional Intelligence* (Bloomsbury: London, 1996).

Goleman, D., *Vital Lies, Simple Truths* (Bloomsbury: London, 1997).

Gumbel, N., *Challenging Lifestyle* (Kingsway Publications: Eastbourne, 1996).

Hancock, M. and Mains, K.B., *Child Sexual Abuse. A Hope for Healing* (Highland: Guildford, 1987).

Holloway, R., *Dancing on the Edge* (Fount: London, 1997).

Hollows, A. and Armstrong, H., eds, *Working With Sexually Abused Boys. An Introduction for Practitioners* (NCB: London, 1989).

La Fontaine, J.S., *Child Sexual Abuse* (Polity Press: Cambridge, 1990).

La Fontaine, J.S., *The Extent and Nature of Organised and Ritual Sexual Abuse* (HMSO: London, 1994).

Lew, M., *Victims No Longer. Men Recovering from Incest and Other Child Sexual Abuse* (Cedar: London, 1993).

Macaskill, C., *Adopting or Fostering a Sexually Abused Child* (Batsford: London, 1991).

MacLeod, M., *Child Protection: Everybody's Business* (Childline/Community Care: Sutton, 1997).

Mendel, M.P., *The Male Survivor. The Impact of Sexual Abuse* (Sage Publications: London, 1995).

Miles, R., *The Children We Deserve* (HarperCollins: London, 1994).

Miller, A., *Thou Shalt Not Be Aware. Society's Betrayal of the Child* (Pluto Press: London, 1985).

Miller, A., *The Drama of Being a Child* (Virago: London, 1995).

Miller, A., *Banished Knowledge. Facing Childhood Injuries* (Virago: London, 1997).

Norwood, R., *Women Who Love Too Much* (Arrow Books: London, 1986).

Parkinson, P., *Child Sexual Abuse and the Churches* (Hodder and Stoughton: London, 1997).

Peck, M.S., *The Road Less Travelled. A New Psychology of Love, Traditional Values and Spiritual Growth* (Rider: London, 1988).

Peck, M.S., *The Different Drum. Community-making and Peace* (Arrow: London, 1990).

Peck, M.S., *Further Along the Road Less Travelled* (Simon and Schuster: London, 1993).

Peck, M.S., *A World Waiting to be Born. The Search for Civility* (Arrow: London, 1994).

Peck, M.S., *The Road Less Travelled and Beyond* (Rider: London, 1997).

Phillips, M., *All Must Have Prizes* (Little, Brown and Company: London, 1996).

Renvoize, J., *Innocence Destroyed. A Study of Child Sexual Abuse* (Routledge: London, 1993).

Sinason, V., *Mental Handicap and the Human Condition. New Approaches from the Tavistock* (Free Association Books: London, 1992).

Smith, D.J., *The Sleep of Reason. The James Bulger Case* (Arrow: London, 1995).

Tate, T., *Children for the Devil. Ritual Abuse and Satanic Crime* (Methuen: London, 1991).

Waterhouse, L., ed, *Child Abuse and Child Abusers. Protection and Prevention* (Jessica Kingsley: London, 1996).

Yancey, P., *Where is God When it Hurts?* (Marshall Pickering: London, 1990).

BULLYING
WHAT *CAN* PARENTS DO?

Bullying is a widespread social problem, both in school and at home. Bullying does not just involve a minority of children. It affects all of us in one way or another - and not simply as bullies or victims.

Bullying covers a vast range of behaviour, and parents themselves are often caught up in it. Kevin Brown's research has shown that parents and teachers who get involved often do so in ways that make the problem worse. The common forms of intervention used by parents and teachers fall into the categories of rescuing, indifference and punishment. The author shows how each of these perpetuates the bullying cycle.

Kevin Brown presents a comprehensive re-examination of the bullying phenomenon. He argues that we need to grasp what it means to see ourselves as people of worth. In establishing our own value we are less likely to become either victims or bullies. Through an understanding of Jesus' mission we can find a sense of self-worth which we need to pass on to our children.

KEVIN BROWN has substantial experience as a social worker and educationalist. He is now a freelance trainer and author living in Penicuik, Scotland. He has written extensively about bullying in schools, and has produced a novel, videos and classroom material on this subject. He and his wife have five children.

Bullying – What *CAN* Parents do?
Kevin Brown
ISBN 1 85424 361 6   £7.99

Available from your local Christian Bookshop.
In case of difficulty contact Monarch Books,
Concorde House, Grenville Place, Mill Hill, London NW7 3SA

MONARCH
B O O K S